MARTINS FERRY P.L. (MFP)
3 3667 00307 4595

BISON
BOOKS

D1561355

WINTER

CORNELIUS OSGOOD

INTRODUCTION TO THE BISON BOOKS EDITION BY

Nick Jans

With Decorations by Jean Day

UNIVERSITY OF NEBRASKA PRESS
LINCOLN AND LONDON

Manufactured in the United States of America

First Nebraska paperback printing: 2006

Library of Congress Cataloging-in-Publication Data
Osgood, Cornelius, 1905–
Winter / Cornelius Osgood; introduction by Nick Jans; with decorations by Jean Day.—Bison books ed.
p. cm.
Originally published: New York: W. W. Norton, 1953.
ISBN-13: 978-0-8032-8623-8 (pbk.: alk. paper)
ISBN-10: 0-8032-8623-6 (pbk.: alk. paper)
1. Osgood, Cornelius, 1905– 2. Pioneers—Northwest Territories—Mackenzie—Biography. 3. Ethnologists—Northwest Territories—Mackenzie—Biography. 4. Frontier and pioneer life—Northwest Territories—Mackenzie. 5. Outdoor life—Northwest Territories—Mackenzie—History—20th century. 6. Wilderness survival—Northwest Territories—Mackenzie—History—20th century. 7. Winter—Northwest Territories—Mackenzie—History—20th century. 8. Athapascan Indians—Northwest Territories—Mackenzie—History—20th century. 9. Mackenzie (N.W.T.)—Description and travel. 10. Great Bear Lake (N.W.T.)—Description and travel. I. Title.
F1096.O8 2006
917.19'3042—dc22 2005023819

This Bison Books edition follows the original in beginning chapter 1 on arabic page 13; no material has been omitted.

NICK JANS

Introduction

It's a premise old as Thoreau: city slicker moves to wilderness, communes with the natural world, and finds inner peace—or at least some ray of enlightenment. In the century and a half since *Walden* was penned, that prototypical American masterpiece has become a template for dozens of books, ranging from incisive and moving to eminently forgettable. At first glance, Cornelius Osgood's *Winter* might seem to fall into that second category—published in England fifty years ago, a memoir pieced together from an old man's journals and recollections of a single winter he spent living alone in an Athapaskan Indian settlement on the remote arctic shores of Canada's Great Bear Lake in 1928. Given that frame of reference, *Winter* could be easily mistaken for a post-Victorian adventure saga, bogged down in florid verbiage and ethnocentric attitude, and offering little insight beyond a sigh of relief that such style and world view are fading in the rearview mirror.

But instead, Osgood's book emerges like a long-abandoned cabin from a snowdrift, immaculately crafted and both timely and timeless, ready for the contemporary reader to inhabit. I'm not by nature a glad-hander, and as a twenty-five-year resident of bush Alaska and a student of northern literature, I'm well aware of the heap of mediocre stuff out there—some of it clumsily written if authentic; some acclaimed in literary or popular circles but vapid and gee-whiz to anyone who's actually lived for a few years beyond cities and roads. *Winter*, though, is a masterpiece of its kind, as true a depiction of life in the far north as any ever written. And Osgood's spare, honest voice is such an integral part of the story that tale and teller are inseparable. His style is surprisingly graceful and in places elevates to a lyrical, poetic intensity: "Here a gray and silver world, lonely and desolate with the moon staring above the black line of the earth's edge, drew in upon me shivering in the wind" (14).

If you're anticipating a tale of epic proportions, replete with polar bears and packs of wolves, cliff-hanging drama and exotic Native ritual, look elsewhere. From its outset, *Winter* is an unassuming chronicle of the author's experiences and the everyday life in and around a tiny Indian settlement known as the Fishery; Osgood, as a young ethnographer employed by the Canadian government, newly arrived by the last steamboat of the season, realizes that his proposed study of local Native life is doomed to fail. What's more, his meager outdoor skills and supplies may not be enough to carry him through the coming winter. But since there won't be another supply boat up the McKenzie until the following summer, he really doesn't have much choice.

Driven by the can-do, open spirit that brought him there in the first place and aided from the start by the locals whose matter-of-fact generosity is almost overwhelming, he sets out to secure the basics of survival: food, shelter, and firewood, and the equipment such gathering requires. He muddles through early attempts at fishing with a gill net in the lake, learns by trial and error to drive the dog team he's bought, and suffers the indignity of his struggles being scrutinized by amused residents. He's all but adopted by an effusive trapper named Pierre and a white trader, Bill, both of whom are married to local Indian women. Bill lends him a derelict cabin and others in the little community pitch in, helping or teaching the newcomer as if he were one of their own. And in his recounting of his everyday toils, trials, and tribulations, Osgood paints a portrait of remote bush life seldom equaled. While of course the focus is often through the lens of self—it is, after all, a first-person narrative—he somehow manages to distill the very essence of each and every being he encounters: the volatile, antic Pierre; his stoic moose-hunting wife, Celine; Peter, the superior sled dog who often shames him with a glance; the intellectually starved, ragged priest at the Fort; warm-hearted Bill, whose abrupt, icy withdrawal of friendship catches both Osgood and the reader off guard. And not forgotten are the Indians of the settlement, whom the author somehow manages to cast as individuals in incisive, thumbnail sketches while giving us a clear-eyed vision of their lives, free of the cloying idealism or cultural smugness that characterizes so many other accounts. From the old woman sleeping in a crowded tent who spits tobacco juice over his thawing dinner biscuits to the little girl dying bravely of tuberculosis and the card-playing lake trout fishermen who welcome him to their spring camp, each is simply, for better or worse, a person. And by book's end, we feel we've somehow met them all ourselves, sat around the stove drinking tea, and shared moments that artfully sum up their lives:

> The old lady chattered away completely at her ease, only stopping to produce a short-stemmed pipe and ask me for tobacco which made the others laugh. When I gave it to her she convulsed the girls by the statement that now I had become her only sweetheart. Her old face, gnarled like spruce root, wrinkled up the faint lines tattooed in blue upon her chin, and her eyes twinkled with the thought of years gone by. I gave her a spool of thread and said she would have to make me moccasins so that I could go hunting in the spring. She nodded her head and moaned softly, as though a price in labor had always been the burden of her joys. (95)

Osgood describes the largest and most silent character of all—the landscape—with equal skill. Again, his words are chosen with taut economy, offering just enough quick-sketched detail that we find ourselves envisioning the endless expanse of Great Bear Lake and the bitter darkness of fifty below zero, looking over the author's shoulder as he points toward this cabin or that line of trees and filling in the gaps with our own imagination. There are no ornate descriptions and seldom a false note; Osgood's prose is lean and unsentimental as the land itself, and his instinct for sensory imagery—the sights, sounds, textures and scents of northern life—is huge:

> By the middle of January, the temperature which had been dipping each few days dropped to minus forty, holding the settlement in its stiff grasp. All wind ceased and one's breath purred from the freezing of exhaled moisture. There was no other constant save the crackling of smooth surfaces on the saltlike snow. The moon came up over half the southern sky, first yellow, then shrinking into an enormous pearl. Smoke from the houses rose straight like pale-blue streamers, gradually evaporating into the translucent heavens. One's fingers numbed in seconds and burned at the touch of a dog chain. The people huddled in their houses, only going outside to relieve themselves. (169–70)

If the people and landscape Osgood encountered form the musculature of the story, the spine of *Winter* is made of precise, carefully detailed descriptions that could practically serve as a subsistence manual for the neophyte—how to thread a gill net under the ice, swing a short ax, steer a loaded toboggan, feed and rest dogs at proper intervals on a long run—what Osgood calls "the little things, perhaps the unimportant things, the predicaments in the process of learning to stay alive" (11). Clearly these matters were the opposite of "unimportant" to Osgood (his writing is often tinged by such subtle irony) or to anyone who's wrestled with freezing hands, miscalculated a treacherous stretch of ice, or lost the thread of a snowed-in trail. Life in this landscape depends on mastery of precise skills, level judgment, and a toughness, both physical and mental, that evolves only through experience. These hard-won bits of knowledge are, in the words of poet William Carlos Williams, "the thing itself." Without them, the book would ring hollow, which it most assuredly does not. Osgood had clearly been there and done that—a remarkably complete immersion for one who spent such a brief time in that landscape. No less remarkable is the clarity of his recollections, the precision with which he set down and summed up what passed before him.

And scattered through the narrative are subtle but profound observations that show Osgood not only lived the life on a personal level, but cast a far wider net to capture (as he put it in his gorgeously worded introduction) "the truth about a country at a peculiar time—some truth about animals and men" (11). Consider, for example, this summation of Fort McKenzie's layout: "The Police buildings stood at the northern end on the highest level with the Catholic Mission in the center and the white-fenced Hudson's Bay Company post finishing the arc . . . These three well-kept headquarters overlooked the thirty-odd cabins below, just as in large measure their occupants dominated the lives of the remaining inhabitants" (155). As in so many places throughout the book, Osgood manages to impart flashes of insight that seem to arise organically from the narrative flow. Shown rather than told, the reader is both included in these discoveries and given space to arrive at personal meaning. The author's restraint from judgment, and his willingness to allow ambiguity to resonate, add to the richness of the experience. We never know, for example, if Pierre or Bill were unjustified in their eventual shunning of the young Osgood; he neither condemns them nor excuses himself, only including us vicariously in his pain, occasionally reflecting, "without emotion . . . on the human mechanism by which men socially repudiate their neighbors" (192).

The greatest triumph of *Winter*, perhaps, is Osgood's ability to capture with unflinching accuracy the actual psychological experience of living through that hard season, wrapped in a profound aloneness that few of us ever will know. Darkness and isolation gnawed at the edges of his being, exacting a relentless toll; at times, he slid into despair and even teetered on the threshold of sanity, beset by "autistic fantasies . . . inevitable for the isolated immigrant to the arctic" (12): "My feelings coarsened as I kept more and more to myself for there was no place to go. I did not wash my face or clean my dishes . . . I would say to myself, 'For God's sake, do something!' . . . hour after hour I would stay in the little room from which I could not see, alternately dreaming and hating myself" (172).

An outsider might wonder if Osgood's emotional trauma was either played up or a product of a fragile psyche, but as I read his words, two decades of solitary arctic winters weighed once more on my chest, and I recalled my own struggles, and those I witnessed in others. Osgood's portrayal of "torment and heartache" is faithful enough to make me shudder. I remember, too, being swept by the same erotic, loneliness-driven fantasies that beguiled the young Osgood, personified in Neidja, the alluring ice ghost that beckons him on before always sliding just out of reach:

> "Don't your knees get cold?" I said, fascinated by the curves of skin which disappeared beneath her parka.
>
> "Never mind my legs," she answered with a laugh like snow which suddenly slips down a mountain slope in spring.
>
> "Go to sleep so you will love the woods tomorrow."
>
> "Come closer then," I said. She moved beside my bed, and breathing heavily I seemed to see twin stars like sparkling studs of ice flashing and twinkling in the bosom of the sky. (203)

If there is finally a disappointment in Osgood's tale, it lies in its ending, or rather the lack thereof. As the author is returning to the Fishery from a long solo dogsled journey at springtime along the fringe of Great Bear Lake, the narrative suddenly stops with the image of Pierre waving a welcome back to the little settlement that Osgood will soon leave forever. I still don't have a ready answer for the abruptness of Osgood's own departure from his own story, made more disappointing by the fact I didn't want to let go just yet. Given the polished introduction, I was also expecting some sort of quiet but brilliant denouement, smooth and transparent as new ice. On the other hand, maybe the ending is just as Osgood intended it, and as it should be—him forever caught in that moment, on the edge of a place that shaped the rest of his life but was never home.

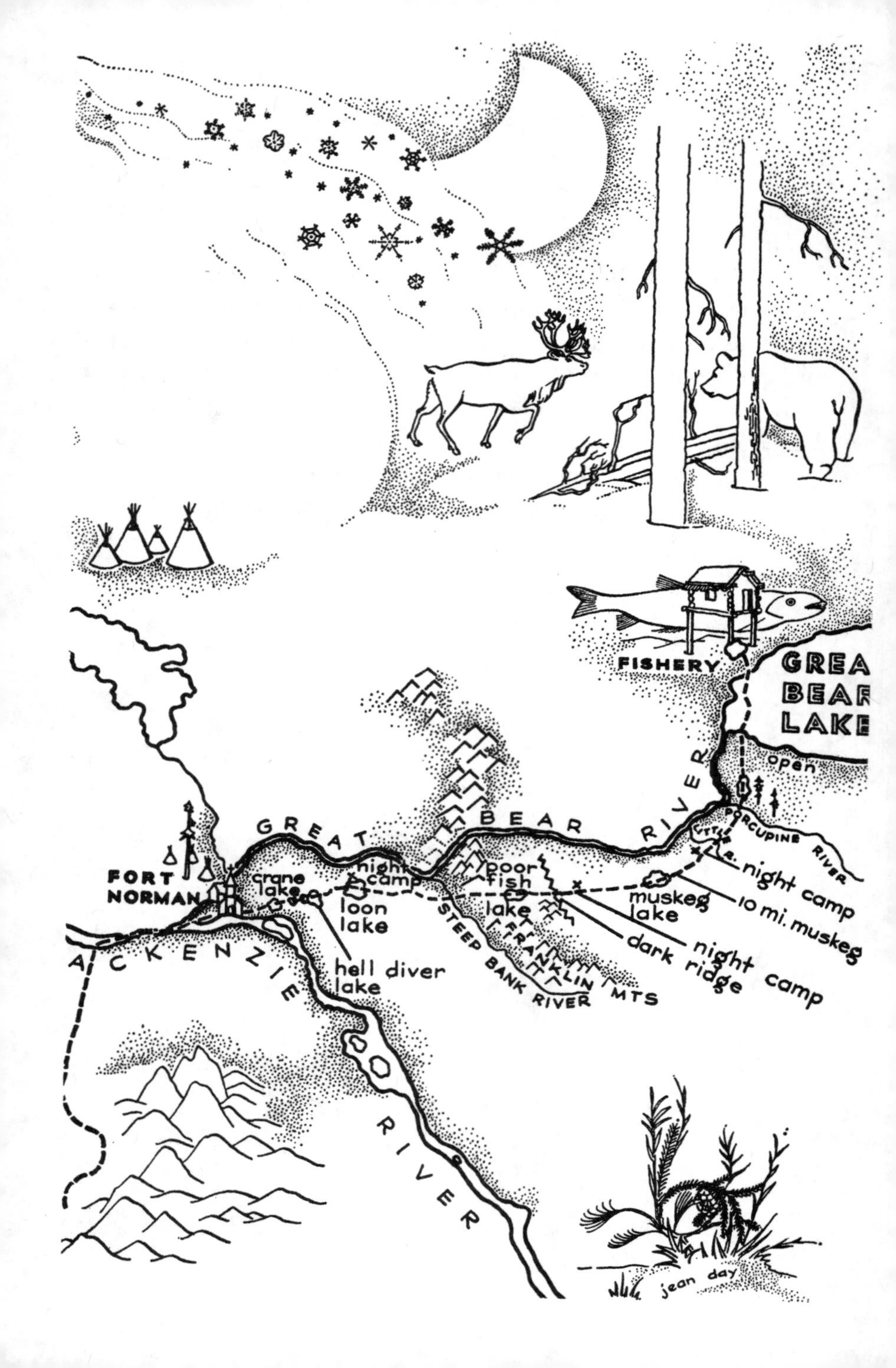

FISHERY
GREAT BEAR LAKE
open
GREAT BEAR RIVER
PORCUPINE RIVER
LITTLE R.
night camp
10 mi. muskeg
FORT NORMAN
crane lake
night camp
loon lake
poor fish lake
muskeg lake
dark ridge
night camp
hell diver lake
STEEP BANK RIVER
FRANKLIN MTS
MACKENZIE RIVER
jean day

ARCTIC OCEAN
GREAT BEAR LAKE
FISHERY
GREAT BEAR RIVER
FORT NORMAN
MACKENZIE RIVE

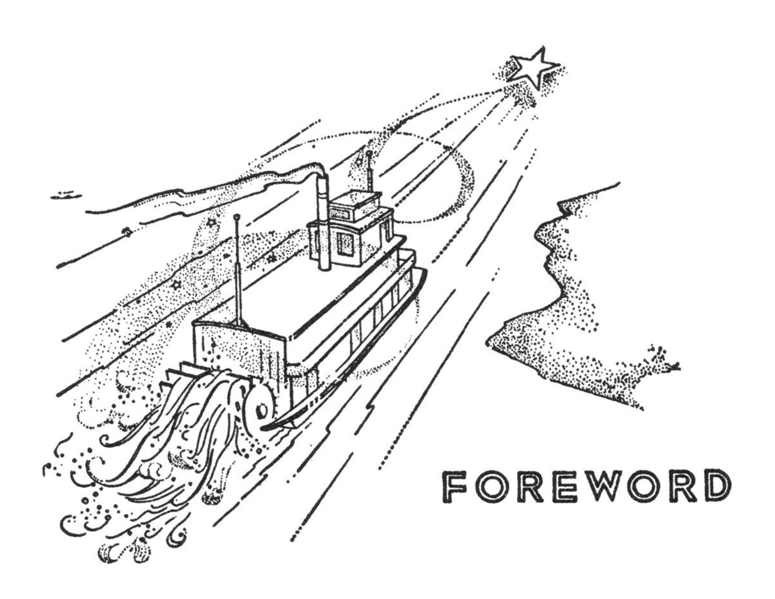

FOREWORD

THERE are experiences in life which are so unusual that one comprehends them only in retrospect. This is an account of such an experience. It was written because truth and beauty can mean more than anything else in the world to human beings and because throughout life I have sought truth and beauty with only a brief glimpse given me here and there. As I look back I see what I did not see when the events occurred many years ago. That time was near an end point in history, an end point of a period when men could drift alone into lands so unknown there were no maps, so desolate one was a law unto oneself, and so far away one could not think of returning in the year one went. The place was Great Bear Lake beyond the frontier of the surging

European migrations which in a few centuries overwhelmed the world and which with recent technological developments have finally made nowhere distant. Lying back of the central arctic coast, this plateau region of Canada with its tremendous basin of fresh water is one of the coldest places on earth. Until twenty-five years ago it had been visited by not more than a few score of Europeans and was the home of small bands of Indians who seem only in recent centuries to have regularly resided there. The chief attractions were the fish in the Lake and the herds of caribou and muskox ranging the adjacent Barren Grounds. But life was too hard and the number of those who failed to survive was greater than those who did. Then early in the decade of the nineteen-thirties came the discovery of valuable minerals, including pitchblende which made Great Bear Lake a sourceland of the atomic bomb.

In that journey to the north which began in the spring of 1928, I did not seek adventure. I went in the role of an ethnographer employed by the Canadian Government to conduct research on the lesser known tribes of the Athapaskan Indians who occupy most of the interior of northwest America. These are the people whose relatives pushed southward perhaps a thousand years ago to become the Navajo and Apache nations of the United States. At almost the beginning of a ten-year program, I had chosen to study a primitive group with which it was most difficult to make contact. After acquiring certain basic information, which I planned to use in the writing of a doctoral dissertation at the University of Chicago, I hoped to proceed with the analysis of more complex societies. Scientifically, the undertaking was a failure. It would have been sensible to have chosen a more favorable locale for my first extended field work. Perhaps I was fortunate to survive the attempt, and in the autumn of 1929 I returned on an old stern-wheeler slowly splashing its way up the Mackenzie.

Although the immediate rewards for anthropology were negligible, they were very great for me. I came to know loneliness as some few men know it, the lovely loneliness of limitless land and sky, of snow and trees. And even more, I came upon the truth about a country at a peculiar time—some truth about animals and men.

There was a reason to tell these things that grew out of the hardship and pain but bitterness shut my mouth. For months I had paddled on the northern rivers, periodically meeting the men who lived alone. I had seen their tracks where they had run away when I approached by dog team. I knew their silent laugh when someone mentioned a book written about the north. It was not their north or mine. I have heard them say, "You know it, you write it!" And at last in a strange way I have.

I have tried to tell the little things, perhaps the unimportant things, the predicaments in the process of learning to stay alive. I have tried to divert the literary power of realistic description to actual experience, to give a precision to detail even sharper than that acceptable as scientific accuracy. A diary has been collated with an almost indelible visual memory to document the changing natural environment. Thus in a sense, this story is a study in the sensitivity of one individual to that environment as experienced between the first snowfall of an arctic winter and the coming of summer. The emphasis lies on human behavior and perceptible things, together with the feelings which are directly related. Individual thoughts appear only intermittently for, in circumstances such as described, one's ideas are almost completely composed of either recollections of what seems long past or anticipations of things to come in a distant future. Inevitable for the isolated immigrant in the arctic are the autistic fantasies which flood the mind when it is weary and pushed so far beyond functioning consciously that only anxiety remains. The presentation of this psychological phenomenon is difficult but certainly should not be construed as a singular example of imagination. In the writing I have tried to achieve a document that is as accurate as words can be. If there is also a melody that one can hear, so much the better.

1

THE snow was white upon the ground and the air blew cold and clean across the Lake. It was the first night I understood what they meant when they said that winter in this far north was never dark. The last weeks of August and on into September I had seen the summer sun disappear earlier, noticeably earlier each evening over the spruce tree fringe of the western ridge, pulling up its silver veil from the water's face until only the yellow eyes blinked between the branches, blinked and then closed leaving blackness.

Now the first white snow reflected a sky of many-layered lights. As the sun rolled its colored ribbons back beyond the mountains, stars darted forth, shone for a brief moment before being lost in the magnitude of those behind. Distance decreased, small hummocks in the muskeg burgeoned forth, the near hills locked arms and came closer driving clumps of willows before them. Here a gray and silver world, lonely and desolate with the moon staring above the black line of the earth's edge, drew in upon me shivering in the wind.

Up from the snow stood five stakes driven into the hard ground below. Around each had been snapped the end of a heavy chain. As I approached, four furry heads raised, lifting lines of tinkling steel links, silvered with frost. Suddenly a huge beast sprang toward me, checked by his chain so late that I could feel his hot breath on my face while his claws ripped threads from my clothes. Thunder and lightning never burst on a peaceful night with such quick fury as the roar from those throats, first staccato sharp, then passing from one to another in a rolling tattoo of growls beaten out with hatred toward all alive, the pitch heightening with the loss of air from the lungs until the quality of frenzy surpassed all others.

The long, braided caribou-skin whip snapped like a dead limb of a tree suddenly broken and fell across the nearest face with white teeth glistening from the open mouth. The head did not flinch, but there was a sudden silence as from surprise —not fear—and almost as though the new sound brought with it a sense of familiar security. The brown eyes stared questioningly while the throat rumbled a warning resonance like overheavy breathing. Here was an animal, bred in the snow from forgotten strains of the wild and the tame, from the cunning and the strong, a dog whose powerful jaws would still seek the enemy's flesh even while collapsing into unconsciousness.

His hair was ivory white all over except for black eyebrows and a cream-colored streak which spread down and off the sides of his nose. His ears were short and drooped like those of an Eskimo dog but he was heavy—close to a hundred pounds—with the powerful shoulders and massive hindquarters of a St. Bernard set into the sinewy body of a wolf. I loved him at sight and was afraid he would bite me.

Suddenly Whitey turned from me and jumped at the dog next to him. The other almost from the first moment of the uproar had concentrated his attack on his companion as though a personal resentment filled him with such bitterness as to make any human irritation an incidental intrusion. The lips drawn back from his sharp incisors transformed his peculiar features into something altogether vicious. The shoulders of the dog were large and powerful but seemed to waste away toward the haunches as though some temporary paralysis had once prevented their full growth, giving him, except for his coloring, the look of a hyena. His coat showed predominantly black filled out with a narrow white gore running up the center of his nose, two white spots more between than above his eyes, a white mouth, chest, feet, and tip to his tail. His ears drooped and had scraggly gray fur projecting from inside. The combination proved unpleasant, principally because of the disharmonic body and the spots which distorted his eyes, but also as the result of the long snarled hair around his throat for which he was called Curly. It was obvious that throughout his whole life he had fought for his position among his fellows, fought on any provocation, wounded or weary, without fear and without consideration for affection or friends.

On the other side of Whitey, another dog was leaping into the air, twisting and pulling at his chain with such crazy contortions that sometimes he lost his balance and fell on his face. His barking shifted over the whole range of dog sounds, from growls to shrill cries thinning out into silence from being too highly pitched. He was the largest of all the animals and the color of a sugar-sprinkled summer lynx. Although he was making more noise than the others together, the inconsistency of his performance showed a lack of purpose and an emotional instability which indicated, despite the fact that all his companions were several years older and he himself not quite three, that he still had in him more of the puppy than superficial observation would suggest. His silly antics made me want to pull his pointed ears, but although playful himself, it would have been a serious mistake to make him mad. Ginger fitted him admirably as a name.

At a more distant point on the circle a fourth dog strained at his leash. His barking had been replaced by a long nasal whine as though he were lonely. To me he was strikingly beautiful, with thick fur glistening like a fox in midwinter. His head was raven black save for a triangle of white running down from its apex between his eyes and gradually widening to encompass the glossy jet nose set in its base. White hair stockings completely encased his forelegs and attached themselves to a collar of the same color reaching to the throat and fastened around the neck in a band with a silver fringe. All the rest of his coat was black except for the hair of his snowy hind feet and tip of his bushy tail. Why he was called Scotty I never knew. He was a large dog, but in lean condition. No one could doubt that by nature he exemplified that remarkable devotion which has allied dogs to man through those centuries since the first wolf whelp grew to trust a two-legged foster parent, a friend who for his part had courageously dared to seek the companionship of a dangerous animal. As I approached, his legs trembled ever so slightly and he twisted his head while watching me steadily. Intense feeling shone through his golden eyes and I felt an uncontrollable desire to warm my face against his hot body.

The remaining stake held a fifth dog. From the others he differed in almost every respect. During the entire commotion he had disturbed himself only to the extent of rising to his feet and shaking himself twice, after which he lay down again with an obvious look of disgust for the whole situation, a prejudice probably combined from castration and an extraordinary intelligence. Certainly he did not consider the fresh snow an ideal bed, a judgment which was understandable since his hair was too short for much protection. In appearance he was no more than a somewhat battered overgrown Boston bull terrier about six years old in a slightly scar-torn white coat. Chance had given him the name Peter but it might have been any other, so overwhelming was his personality. I would have accepted immediately a relationship of intimacy

B

with this alien of the north but when he fixed his eyes upon me, I felt his superiority, his confidence that for himself alone he had found a way of survival through years of bitter hardship, a pride and self-sufficiency not to be shared simply for the asking. Would I be able to do likewise? Previously the challenge of the winter had not seemed so great but in my isolation I felt ignorant and something of a fool. Chilled until my cheeks were stiff, I moved away, smiling through windborn icy tears at the tremendous arctic moon.

2

MY TENT was cold as the fire had died in the tin stove made from a five-gallon gasoline can. The interior of the can was too small for anything but little sticks which burned up quickly, constantly changing the temperature in the eight-by-ten V-shaped enclosure inverted over a thick bed of spruce boughs. Heating proved to be a problem, as concentration on anything else soon chilled me into realizing. Absent-mindedness had been of no significance until the past few days when northwest winds had started dropping the mercury well below freezing. The conceit which had brought me into the situation was at last being faced with consequences for which I was painfully unprepared.

The butcher knife that served all purposes was dull so I filed it inefficiently without removing my heavy mooseskin mittens. Then I picked a straight-grained spruce stick from the pile near the stove, put an end on a log, and proceeded to cut shavings. Beginning near the end, a little strip of wood curled up under the pressure of the knife until it nestled in a tight coil at the bottom. Starting over again just above the first incision, a second sliver rolled down the stick. The third was winding beautifully when the supporting log slipped slightly, twisting the knife so that the three shavings snapped off together. A small matter really, but it beguiled me to cut up a whole stick into a clump of coiled splinters. I chose another piece and started in again.

The dogs had become completely quiet. They were my chief problem because they had to be fed. Every day each one would need at least three or four fresh fish—better say twenty altogether as I also would have to eat. That made two hundred every ten days, six hundred a month, about six thousand before open water came again with the chance to get out of the country. Fortunately, the lake provided a rare supply of scaly inhabitants if one possessed the experience to catch them. I had not wanted to go fishing since I was seven.

My pile of chips had grown considerably. I picked up several of the most perfect and put them under my chin for there was no one to tell that they looked like whiskers. Then I stuffed them into the stove, thick ends first, adding the splinters and a few larger pieces on top. They blazed from the first touch of the match and the flames roared up the four-inch stovepipe which elbowed out through the middle of a metal pie plate sewn into the cloth wall. The fire cheered me and when the tent warmed, I pulled off mittens and brown drill windbreak, stuffing them under my head while I rolled over on top of my eider-down sleeping bag.

If it had not been for the dogs, my mind would have been at ease. Not that anyone could have taken them from me then. They were my dogs and I refused to consider the possibility of living without them. Lying quietly, my memory drifted back over months to the days when I first heard of the dogs. I had come down the Mackenzie River on the steamboat after the breakup of the ice, intending to study the almost unknown group of Indians who hunted over the Barren Grounds surrounding Great Bear Lake. My hope of joining some native family journeying to the interior had soon been destroyed, for with my arrival at the fur trading post, an epidemic descended on the few score of people who had been lured to the River in anticipation of seeing the steamer. For days, men, women, and children lay feverish on the cold sand of the beach, sometimes attacked in their helplessness by their hunger-mad dogs. Many died and the survivors fled, half sick and fearful, not capable of carrying away their customary small burden of supplies. My company would have but contributed to their difficulties as I knew only a few words of their language and they less of mine.

It was at that time I met the Greenland Dane from whom I was to obtain my dogs. He had carefully selected them for an extended trip across the arctic and, having completed his work, he was about to leave the country. With the dogs, it was pointed out, I would find the freedom to travel whenever I wished; they would haul dry timber to warm a camp, pull food from the fish nets, and detach me from a dangerous dependence on some near-starving band of wandering Indians. In short, it was made clear that if I wished to spend the winter away from the trading post, dogs would be a necessity. The dogs had been left across the mountains at the end of the great Lake stretching out hundreds of miles across the tundra. At that place I would find a white man who was married to a native woman. He knew the Indian language and had been in and out of the country for many years. From him I could learn everything that might be needed.

The decision in favor of the dogs became inevitable and thus after several months I had come into the present situation. Unfortunately, this white man named Bill had gone away and although everything that had been said about the dogs appeared unquestionably true, I could not safely approach them.

The fire had become quiet in the stove, a certain sign that it had almost died out. I crawled over the intervening brush and opened the crude door of the can, burning my fingers when it would not come loose. A few red coals glistened like fresh fish gills in the ashes. When some sticks were laid on them and nothing happened, I jammed in more, amused by the puzzle of how many could be fitted into such a small space at one time. It was cold lying on the brush so I replaced the outer garments taken off earlier.

Suddenly little staccato sounds issued from the tin and little flames lighted up the interstices around the door. Something of that pleasure which accompanies the assurance of life in a fire exhilarated me but I had hardly become conscious of my securing sensation before my pulse leaped with excitement. The can had become a little inferno glowing with an intensity which lighted the whole tent. Panic paralyzed me for a minute in the fear that the cloth walls of my shelter would catch fire. The stuffing of dry sticks was too much for the stove to stomach and it disgorged flames like a mythical monster blood-red from head to tail. Desperately I dashed outside. As from a blowtorch, fire shot out a foot from the chimney end. Scooping up a mound of snow on my broad mittens, I rushed back and showered it on the scarlet metal which crackled and sizzled and steamed with resentment. Already receding in fury, the fire quieted and the snow sucked the color from the stove faster than the pupils of my eyes could adjust to the darkness filling the interior of the tent. A feeling of relief preceded that faint sickness which follows sudden fear. The still-stifling heat drove me outside into the night air cursing the stove for dominating my time and emotions.

Everything around me was quiet. The fresh-fallen snow, damp from the autumn sun, had covered all the surface of the ground but the tops of bushes protruded here and there. South a few hundred feet lay the great Lake with a faint line of lapping water on a stony beach. I could just make out a score of Indian cabins less than a mile across the shallow bay to the east. From them I was cut off by a deep water slough just beyond the tent. The slough connected the bay with a little lake that spread out tenuously perhaps a thousand yards into gradually rising land thinly covered by spruce trees. Lonely in the intervening foreground were several simple buildings, ash-gray from the lash of storms on their unpainted surfaces: a gable-roofed, oblong, one-story structure built of rough boards hewn with a broad ax to serve intermittently as warehouse and store; a slightly larger counterpart a few steps on the other side comprising a three-room dwelling; between them and the slough, a cache—a miniature house supported above head height by means of heavy posts; and lastly in the near distance close to the little lake, an undersized log cabin which most recently had served as shelter for a team of dogs.

Such was the Fishery, the single permanent settlement in an area of forty thousand square miles, without a light or a sound save the rhythmic waves of the tremendous tidal Lake. Under its dark water lay hidden the winter's source of food. With anxiety, I entered my cold tent and slept fretfully for dreams of fish.

3

A HEAVY snow had fallen during the night but the temperature had moderated to a little below freezing. The dogs looked cold so as a gesture of friendship I trudged off to the edge of the woods to cut a few spruce saplings from which to make them beds.

The ax I carried was of a type peculiar to the country, having a straight handle about twenty inches long and a hatchet head weighing less than two pounds. It was not the heavy tool of the lumber camp but a precision instrument with a razor-edge which could deliver a whiplike blow when swung single-handed at arm's length. No other object had a value quite so great in the north. Without it, one could not survive alone in the winter. Another trait of the ax demanded respect. It could cut one down, bleeding, helpless in the snow. This possibility brought me no great uneasiness; I merely reflected on it as I swung at a little tree, slicing the trunk nearly through in a single stroke. Never during the summer had I felt nervous about an ax, even if alone and beyond reach of assistance. This innovation had come with the immobilizing snow and the cold. Sometimes I overthrust my aim in unconscious intent not to let the blade glance off the near side of the mark and into my flesh. Then I would tighten my muscles and swing hard and close out of annoyance for my weakness. When I had felled all the pieces I could drag behind me, I set off back to my camp.

The dogs seemed interested at my approach, perhaps hoping that we were about to travel as they had grown restless from being chained in one spot. Leaning the saplings on their butts, I trimmed off the branches, dividing up the sprays of green needles to make a small mattress for each.

Except for short-haired Peter, the reaction of the dogs did not prove particularly rewarding. He, however, immediately walked into the center of his pile, turned around two or three times and settled down with what I interpreted as a grunt of satisfaction. The others paid more attention to me than to the brush and Scotty came out to the end of his six-foot chain wagging his tail. He gave me that friendly inquisitive look with his head slightly twisted. I patted him a little and then he stood up on his hind legs trying to lick me.

The other dogs, except Peter, began stretching themselves and mooing like young calves. It was obvious that they were slightly envious and when I continued stroking Scotty, they began to bark from pure jealousy. I did not like the uproar so I started back to the tent, giving Ginger one pat on the head as I passed. This pleased him for he went up to his stake and urinated on it several times, still watching me happily.

Feeding the dogs was bringing me rapidly into a special relationship with the team. I no longer felt entirely alone, although somewhat more aware of our difficulties for we were running out of food. Our need urgently demanded putting a net into the water as soon as possible.

Among the purchased supplies were a couple of three-pound white twine gill nets, each over a hundred feet long, as well as several balls of cord and larger line to serve as backing. I brought this material out and sat on a box in front of my shelter. The job to be done was simple enough. With a wooden needle one had to pass the cord around the heavier line while catching the meshes at the top of the net so that the latter would hang loosely, then secure meshes and backing together every six or eight feet by binding them with the middle of a two-foot string, leaving the ends of the latter free to tie on the floats. When this was finished, one had only to do the same for the bottom edge, using more short strings to fasten on rock sinkers.

I went to work in good spirits. The undertaking had not progressed far when an old Indian with gnarled hands and a face like spruce bark walked over from the slough to visit me. He squatted near by and took a proffered cigarette which he promptly put into his pocket. I spoke a few words to him in his language but he only nodded since the remarks were nothing more than pleasantries.

The backing of the net moved slowly for somehow this simple procedure had taken on unforeseen complexities. The further it went, the more tangled I became in strings and lines. The old Indian finally made what, since I could not understand a word of it, seemed like a long speech, but he must have recognized my limitations for he afterwards relapsed into silence.

By that time I had become completely fouled in my attempts to back the net. That this Indian should see my incompetence only added to my frustration and I glared at him. For a moment he looked a little uncomfortable and then, perhaps as I relaxed, he smiled, making me laugh in turn. As soon as I had stopped he unbent himself and stepped over to my net. In a few magic minutes he had the net straightened out and was rapidly completing the upper edge, teaching me by example and gestures what one can only learn from experience.

We went on with the work together, talking over the details quite oblivious to the fact that neither of us could understand the other's speech. Hands pointed to things in the distance and a movement of the head to those near by. The muscles of the face questioned or affirmed. Feelings we communicated with our eyes as though we knew that words become only an accessory detail in intimate and important affairs.

The necessary floats I had already prepared from a couple of deadwood poles by chopping them into one-foot lengths and circling their smaller ends with grooves. Then my teacher indicated that he was going to the woodpile near the cache for two heavy buoys for the extremities of the net.

It took quite a while to finish the task because I lacked skill in tying on the rock sinkers but the old man showed me again each time that one slipped from its binding. When we had finished, we laid out the net, layer on layer, on a piece of canvas with the floats all together at the top and the sinkers at the bottom. I thought we were through for the day but my friend clearly indicated that we should go on and set the net.

My mind had been so occupied with preparations, I had hardly given thought to this logical conclusion. Somehow the idea came to me all at once that setting this net was one of the most important acts in my life. Already I had a home of my own, also a family—dogs though they were and still embarrassingly unfamiliar—and now there would be food for us all. With one more act we were to be free. It was like escaping from a maze of snowshoe tracks in which each crossing was an obligation to someone else. Momentary exhilaration intoxicated me, then I sobered quickly. Possibly I would not like this strange land, this life beyond the peripheries of human society. No course appeared, however, but to go on until perhaps from some vantage point I could see a satisfactory return to my fading world of social responsibility. As I pondered, the old man looked at me surprised but I apologized with a smile for my distraction.

We picked up the canvas with the net and carried it down to his canoe. Then we brought aboard the log buoys and the anchors. Pushing off, we paddled out of the slough a short distance into the bay. My Indian companion had foreseen in his mind the exact spot for the nět and we stopped on it as though it stood out like a scrub spruce on the Barrens. Over went one anchor with a buoy and I fed out the net as he propelled us shorewards. The last splash left a long line of sticks bobbing on the blue swells.

My companion put me ashore near the tent and I started to thank him but realized there was nothing to be said. Without a word he pulled away in the canoe and soon disappeared around the point toward the Indian village.

Night was falling and I took a bag of fish over to my dogs. They knew their feeding time and began to jump and bark with the distinctive sounds peculiar to the immediate anticipation of food. Their voices were sometimes sharp, sometimes heavy, but usually short except for occasional drawn-out whines. Although their enthusiasm filled the air, it was a joyful noise which neither man nor animal at the Fishery felt as disturbing. Had they barked with anger, or jealousy, or fear, the whole community would have been aroused and their cries picked up by scores of dogs between our camp and the farthest Indian cabin.

I stood watching them and in a moment irresistibly began to talk.

"What's the matter, Scotty, are you hungry?"

"Oo-o-o," came the answer from the stretched out neck.

"Keep still, Ginger!" to one who had almost gone crazy in anticipation of eating.

"Shut up, all of you!"

They seemed surprised but kept quiet except for an intermittent nasal "hu-u-u." Taking fish out of the bag, I threw one to each dog in turn who caught it in his mouth. Sometimes they appeared to swallow a fish nine or ten inches long in two gulps. Scotty and Peter preserved a slightly more fastidious approach but disposed of the piece in less than a minute. When all had finished I threw each dog another fish. By the time they had a third, their rapacity had died down. I told them that they could have no more because our supply had been eaten up but that I expected fresh fish from the bay very soon. I chose to believe that they looked happy at the prospect and in any event, being assured that dinner was over, they began to sniff in the snow for any scraps which had dropped from their mouths while gulping their meal. It was clearly not very profitable so they proceeded to walk around, their hair bristling, periodically urinating on their posts. After a few minutes of this kind of promenading, each of the dogs, in chance order, walked to the end of his chain and relieved himself. This became most certainly the concluding part of an evening ceremonial, just as the approach of fish indicated its beginning. For them the excitement of the day was over and they sat on their haunches or lay down according to their mood. Except by Peter, I observed that the brush beds were being disregarded. The temperature rested only a little below freezing and the dogs with long hair were more comfortable in the snow.

As I set off for my tent, I stroked Whitey gently on the head. He stood perfectly still, without showing any reaction. Intuitively I knew that he would become my favorite if he would only love me.

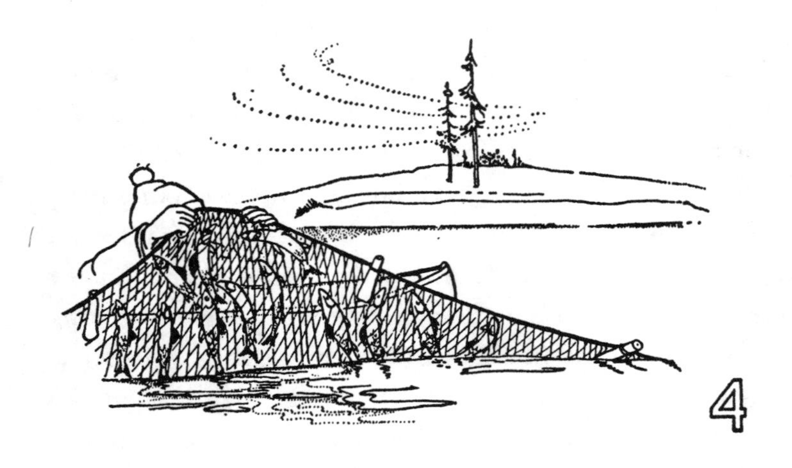

4

THE wind usually blew from the northeast in the morning and shifted to the southwest with the approach of evening, leaving the late afternoon relatively calm and quiet in which to visit the fish nets. I had waited all day for the opportunity, preparing sticks with which to hang the expected harvest. Some Indians had come to inspect the stranger's camp and one of the older women offered to accompany me fishing, in part as a friendly gesture but also out of curiosity as to what results a new net would bring in its particular location. The potential catch, highly variable in time and place, apparently took precedence in every discussion at the Fishery.

Except for being slightly cold, I enjoyed the experience of visiting a fish net as I was thoroughly familiar with canoes and had already absorbed into my subconscious the deep-seated pleasure of accumulating food that passed directly from hand to mouth, food not purchased by intervening labor, or even acquired as a special or superfluous enterprise, but food without which there was hunger for me and my family of dogs.

We lifted the net along the gunwales and here and there plucked a slippery silver whitefish weighing about one and one-half pounds which had caught its scarlet gills in the diamond meshes of white thread. Thumb and forefinger sunk into the soft apertures behind the head, then a twist, and the fish was loose, its yellow eyes expressionless behind a small quivering mouth. The bottom of the canoe was filling with a shining load of flapping tails sparkling in the sunlight.

Half dreaming, I pulled the net, clawing the meshes to reach its lower edge. Of an instant, the threads cut into my fingers as though some monster from the depths had decided to strip the net from my hands. The canoe rocked slightly, causing the woman to yell in such terror that I almost lost my balance and capsized our craft from the double surprise.

She shouted instructions in language I could not understand but the problem had become obvious so as soon as I had regained my composure, I proceeded carefully to get my free hand on the bottom backing of the net, therewith looping the catch as though pulling the edges of a hammock over it. Having thus confined it, I drew it to the surface. Confronted face to face with the creature, my astonishment was greater than before. With complete intimacy, it opened a mouth into which

I could put my head. Obviously it was not possible to lift such a thrashing live weight out of the water but I had no intention of letting it escape.

The Indian woman by this time screamed constantly at me and I could see that her annoyance was based on the fact that the struggling fish would tear the net to pieces, a process it had already well begun.

I judged the captive to be one of the large species of trout commonly ascribed to the great lakes of the far north and certainly a considerable supply of food if we could only land it. I could not think while the woman was making such noise so I said, "God damn it, shut up!" which was evidently translated "Come here!" as she immediately quieted down and crawled over the whitefish to where I was sitting in the stern. Without hesitating she picked up a loose wood float lying in the bottom of the canoe and as I, realizing her intention, pulled up the fish, she struck it over the head until it was dizzy. This procedure pleased me immensely and I was so relieved by a solution, so simple when once understood, that I took the float from her hand and began beating the fish by myself. At this she seemed satisfied and amused.

Together we hauled the net into the boat, then untangled the fish which stretched about four feet long, fat like a month-old bear. Even my companion regarded it with amazement. We finished clearing the net and paddled back toward the Fishery to show off our catch.

With a short piece of cord attached to a stick, which I pushed through the trout's gills and out of its mouth, I tied the fish and carried it over my back to the cache where I hoisted it up to the end of a crossbeam. Everyone around came to see it, voicing considerable admiration as it weighed between forty and fifty pounds which is large for a specimen of its kind.

I offered a piece to the wife of the store owner but she bluntly refused it, walking off home with her children following. On several occasions I had noticed her face which was patterned after features one sees in Leonardo's "Mona Lisa." She was a slim woman and many people would have considered her beautiful. Toward me she was distant which I regretted if only because she spoke English capably. Somewhat affected by the rejection of my prize, I returned to the canoe.

Besides the trout, I had sixty-seven small whitefish and two ling. The liver and eggs of the ling, sometimes called loche, have a fine flavor and are considered a great delicacy by gourmets, but the flesh itself is soft and pulpy which makes it particularly difficult to extract from a net with hands numbed by the cold. Filling a sack with the whitefish, I took them up under the nearly empty fish racks which were constructed of heavy posts with connecting beams on top in two parallel lines. At intervals of about two and one-half feet, strong spruce poles had been laid across the beams higher than one could reach from the ground. Just above the tail of each fish, I drove through the blade of a butcher knife, using the hole thus made to string the catch on the willow sticks previously prepared. With fifteen silver bodies spaced a little apart on a willow, I stood on a box and hung the ends of the stick over cross poles of the rack. The stick sagged slightly; there was always the danger of its sagging too much and slipping to the ground where any stray animal would steal the fish. When I had put up three sticks full, I took the rest of the fish home.

The problem which would worry the whole community during approaching weeks had been explained to me. Although Bear Lake holds an inexhaustible supply of food, obtaining it at certain seasons proves nearly impossible. The most difficult time occurs during the freezing of the ice in the fall. Gradually the edges of the Lake solidify while the ice encroaches further out into the bays. The surface has not strength to support the fisherman who would set nets beneath the ice, yet one cannot navigate in a canoe. Before the ice "makes" as they say, the nets must be pulled or they will be lost. Hence one asks, "Shall I pull my nets today?"

After one does, a fall storm may soon blow up and great waves roll shorewards, breaking into bits the light sheet of fresh ice which takes several quiet days to form. A repetition of such circumstances easily leads to starvation among the Indians. The Fishery takes its advantage in having the maximum period of open water available as the tide causes a current to run with such force, in and out of the slough between the bay and the adjoining little lake, that the near-by shores have open water longer than any other section. The slough itself freezes late, but encloses too small an area in which to accumulate sufficient fish for the community. The possibility of my acquiring enough dog feed to last over the freeze-up seemed poor and my thoughts constantly returned to this difficulty.

The afternoon's experience, however, left me happy and optimistic about the future. The dogs smelled the fresh fish, which still slapped each other in the bag, and showed undeniable appreciation of the feast I had promised to supply. After being fed they were friendlier than ever and I realized that our relationship had already reached the stage of mutual trust, at least within the range of our limited contact.

By the time I had built a fire in the stove and started to prepare my dinner, it was already late. I put on a pail of water to boil and filleted two of the whitefish, cutting my finger slightly when the knife broke through a backbone under pressure. Then I tossed the fillets into the boiling water. Of all tasks, that of cooking solitary meals appealed to me the least. I envied the dogs their direct approach to food and found myself growing more careless each week in my own preparations. Eating fish every day became monotonous. The fish tasted well enough but the limitation in the variety of a dinner annoyed me. Fish as an appetizer I could appreciate, in a soup I could regard it as truly something for the connoisseur, as an entrée more than acceptable, for the icy water of the lake supplied an unsurpassed quality. It was having fish for dessert to which it proved difficult to adjust.

Among my supplies for the winter I had transported five cans of preserved fruit—two peaches, two pineapple, and a tin of cherries—but my attitude toward these symbols of civilization had developed into almost worship, and the idea of consuming them I viewed as a sacramental rite. Therefore I went on eating fish.

5

THE temperature had dropped ten degrees and there was little to induce me to step out of my sleeping bag into the freezing air of the tent. Visiting the fish net had become a cold and discouraging occupation. The catch had decreased intensifying my uneasiness as to whether we would have enough fish to last over the period of the "making" of the ice.

As I lay in my bed daydreaming, Bill's son, a lad of seven, put his head between the flaps of the tent and asked if I wanted to go with his mother and aunt to cut wood on the other side of the little lake.

Welcoming the diversion, I invited him inside and he immediately laid a fire in the tin stove, cutting shavings with an unconscious facility which aroused my envy. He told me that they planned to fell trees on the far hillside, taking the large freight canoe which could carry a considerable number of logs.

I pulled on my pants while the water heated, the tent having warmed in the period of a few minutes. We made a cup of tea and drank it, nibbling on a piece of dryfish between times. The boy had a smooth, sensitive face but, following the custom of the Indians of the country who are usually shy on first acquaintance, talked little. After putting on mooseskin moccasins over my heavy wool socks and adding a pair of rubbers, I picked up my windbreak, mittens, and ax in preparation for the excursion. Dressing required no effort, as like most men in the country, I slept in heavy two-piece underwear, socks, and shirt, all woven of wool.

We walked down to the slough where the women waited, the boy's mother with a black silk handkerchief around her head while her sister wore one of reddish-orange, the color of the inside of a trout freshly cut and drying in the sun. They had brought a bag of lunch and obviously looked forward to the expedition as to a picnic.

Paddling across the lake consumed little time or effort. Cecille, the girl with the bright headdress took an ax and set out with me up the sparsely treed slope looking for deadwood. How to be certain in a marginal case whether a tree had dried enough to burn when split for a small stove still puzzled me. The larger the burner, of course, the greener the wood could be. I tried to cover my perplexity by calling to the boy and telling him it was part of his responsibility to select the trees to be cut. If I thought this would intrigue him I was mistaken for he took the assignment simply as another task. Soon I realized that although gauging a tree had long become effortless for him, to find dry wood so near the settlement required considerable search. In a little while he located a few and I felled and cleaned them of branches.

When I had nearly finished the second tree, I heard a cry of fright from the boy's mother who had joined her sister cutting further down the bank. I ran down the rough slope to them as fast as I could. Cecille sat on a log moaning while her sister held her hands to her blanched face, horrified. The front of one of Cecille's legs had been slit open to the bone, leaving two bulging flaps of skin with edges at least fives inches long hanging over at each side. The flat whiteness of the tibia between the masses of brilliant red flesh fascinated me. The cut had been made as though by a surgeon's scalpel, the knife-like blade of the ax by some good fortune just shaving the bone. I rolled the flaps of skin back in place and bound the leg carefully with a strip of petticoat.

By the time I had finished, my mind began to dwell on what should be done next. The wound needed disinfecting and eight or ten stitches at least. Before I had tied the last knot in the bandage, the two women who had previously made hardly a sound, broke out into laughter. One tittered first, then the other, until both leaned over convulsed with emotion.

I suggested that we had better return home to dress the cut but they laughed more and started to make preparations for lunch. At least, it augured well to have a patient in a good humor so I tramped on up the hill to bring in the logs that had been readied.

This occupied me for quite a while. Lifting one end of a heavy log onto one shoulder, I worked my way down to its middle point where, I becoming a human fulcrum, the tree trunk would slowly raise itself into horizontal position. With the load balanced, I slowly set off down the slope, treading gingerly like a lynx for fear of twisting an ankle under the heavy weight and prepared to heave the log sidewise lest it crush me if I slipped.

By the time I had completed two trips, roasted fish on sticks were waiting beside the fire and a pail of tea had been made by throwing a handful of the leaves into boiling water and allowing them to brew so strong that the bitterness stuck to the top of one's mouth.

Best of all, Cecille passed great slices of freshly made bread that tasted to me like cake. Whenever I even smelled bread I knew that of all foods, I missed it the most. I would promise myself to learn to bake some but the next day when the yeasty aroma had slipped from memory, I was too lazy.

As we completed our meal, I noticed the boy throwing bits of food into the fire. The women, realizing that I had observed his behavior, giggled. I asked him why he did it but he became embarrassed, stood up, and walked a short distance away. At first the women insisted they knew no explanation but from their laughter and sly looks it became quite apparent that they did. Finally, after much teasing one told me a story that she said she had heard as a girl.

Once long ago a man who was hunting killed a moose. Then he made camp and built a fire. Soon afterwards the spirits of his brothers who had been killed in a war came to him and said, "Why do you not see us and give us something to eat?" But he could not see them because they were spirits, nor could they take the meat. Then he dropped some of his food in the fire and the spirits ate it. Ever since, when the Indians notice the peculiar hissing that occurs when a pocket of moisture heats in a burning log, they throw in bits of food for the dead.

After the meal I went back to carry in my last piece of timber. When I had brought it to the shore I discovered that Cecille, despite her injury, had engaged in trimming one of the trees she had cut down.

We filled the freight canoe and climbed aboard the logs to paddle back to the slough. I insisted on washing out Cecille's gash with a silver nitrate solution but at having it sewn up she definitely balked so I bound it carefully with gauze.

As a substitute, seemingly in reaction to my desire to be helpful, it was suggested that I might split some wood for the kitchen. I piled the logs we had brought and selecting the largest, sawed it into suitable lengths. It lacked much of being thoroughly dry and I had trouble in splitting the sections. My ax wedged into the wood and almost twisted out of my hand when I brought ax and wood together crashing down on another log. Everyone but me slyly evinced amusement at my predicament and when a visitor paddled up saying that a canoe had just arrived from the Mackenzie, I decided to go across to the Indian village to discover if there might be news from the outside world. The visitor promised to take me if I dared to squat in the bow of his single-seated craft built like an undecked Eskimo kayak. Content, I threw a few fish to my dogs and we shoved off.

The new arrival was a French Canadian by the name of Pierre. He told me his name and his origin was unmistakable from the strong dialectic flavor of his words. Pierre had a lithe, slight body full of nervous energy and twinkling eyes in a smiling face, constantly askew to keep off the smoke from the hand-rolled cigarette which hung limply from the corner of his mouth. He greeted me on the beach with effusiveness and a touch of emotional exhaustion like a Latin who has just broken his last bottle of wine. He briefly summarized his journey from the trading post on the Mackenzie, told me that his wife had lost a child at birth a few days before, and wanted to know if I had any whiskey. Discovering that I did not, his face drooped for a moment, then flashed back into a smile while he asked me to come to his shack for a cup of tea. Bill, he reported, was only a day behind him and Bill surely would have a bottle cached somewhere.

His cabin consisted of a single large room with an old iron bed, some tables, and a barrel stove. He explained that the house belonged to his father-in-law, who had the reputation of being the best hunter among the Indians, except perhaps for his own wife who could do even better. Believing what Pierre said had little to do with my liking for him. His warmth captured me and I soon discovered that for each person that he favored, only superlatives could express his devotion.

His wife lay resting on the bed in the corner shadows. I could scarcely distinguish her face in the dusk but she smiled at me once. Pierre went on talking about her, quite oblivious to any need for personal reticence. After a little she got up and cooked us some excellent supper although I protested at her troubling out of consideration for her recent accouchement. This only made Pierre laugh and he explained with repetitions and elaborations that just a few hours' rest was necessary after an Indian girl gave birth to a child—indeed, his Celine did not need even so many. Intermittently he asked confirmation for his statements from his wife who paid no attention until he began to shout. Then she smiled at him.

True to form, Pierre suddenly became solicitous, insisting that his wife go to bed, complained to her about her overworking, and almost broke into tears. His imploring left no more effect than his previous commentary but when she finished the dishes, she returned to her bed where she began to nurse a baby about a year old which I noticed for the first time.

Pierre and I discussed the problems of fishing and then, following his lead, women, about whom he seemed to know an extraordinary amount. As it became very late, Pierre gave me a blanket and I went to sleep on the floor, happier with my new-found friend than I had been in many weeks.

6

WE WAKENED late the next morning to find that Celine and her child had left the house. Pierre took some hot water off the stove and washed his face after which he handed me the towel. I followed his example, realizing while doing so that I had not thought of cleaning my face for several days.

We walked outside and saw Celine returning from the beach. She had been out in the canoe with the child, setting a fish net. She cooked our breakfast and as I watched her movements, I became aware of an energy and efficiency rarely to be found in a human being. She ostensibly accomplished several separate tasks at once giving the picture of a speeded-up cinema from which every waste scene had been eliminated.

When we sat down at the table Pierre recounted the difficulties of which I had unburdened myself, she listening sympathetically the while, clearly not understanding all of his words but responding sensitively whenever she caught the gist of my problems. Her husband, as he lost himself in the spell of his own emotions, reached a point where he was promulgating laws to prevent such a tragic existence as fate had unmercifully brought down upon me, alone and unprotected in the arctic. As usual, having run the gamut of his feelings he began to laugh.

Celine, however, had absorbed some truth from his peroration and began to ask short, sharply stated questions which her husband as well as I could not comprehend until she added a sprinkling of English words. She bluntly ordered Pierre to help me put down my other net at once and he confided when his wife stepped outside for wood that she had agreed to make some winter overclothes for me if I would bring as material a Hudson's Bay blanket and half a tanned mooseskin. Such solicitude touched me, and Pierre, immediately affected, repeated over and over "She ees a woman, the very bes' in the whole worl'!" With this opinion, I had no reason to disagree.

When Celine came in with sticks for the stove, my problems seemed forgotten for nothing more was said and she sat down on the bed to sew. As she did not look up, I had the opportunity to observe her closely. Her mooseskin moccasins showed wear and the flaps were bound around strong straight legs encased in thick black cotton stockings largely covered by a dark cotton skirt which bunched around the hips suggesting a heavy petticoat beneath. Over sturdy shoulders she had a tightly buttoned gray wool sweater with a red collar and bands at the wrists. Little of her black hair escaped under the matching silk kerchief tied with a knot over her forehead. Her single ornament was a gold wedding ring. The costume could serve as a model for those worn by all the women of the settlement, each garment, save for the moccasins, purchased with furs at the trading post.

Superficially the bright clay-colored face with heavy but harmonic proportions, the slightly Mongoloid eyes and the snow-white teeth might also have failed to distinguish her from the other Indians, but anyone who had looked twice could recognize the deep security behind the sable eyes and the determination in her high cheek bones. It was a face that could be merciless or infinitely kind.

In the midday light, it was possible to see the interior of the cabin clearly. Above the bed had been pinned two unframed religious chromos and adjacent to them a small cheese-box was nailed, the open top outwards, thereby supplying a pair of shelves to preserve knickknacks of one kind or another. A small watch, which I guessed had not run for years, hung from a nail near by and a cardboard calendar had been tied to the bedposts, partially concealed by the draping folds of a mosquito bar unused since summer.

All around the walls, spikes held a miscellany of articles including caps, slippers, cooking utensils, an Indian tambourine, and several old calendars superimposed one upon another. There was a baking drum set into the stovepipe and several crude tables placed between the three small windows were bordered with brightly patterned oilcloth. Empty boxes functioned as chairs. At its least, it was a home and, considering that it contained the only iron bed, probably the best-furnished cabin in the settlement.

Pierre had been talking endlessly about the trapping prospects which, since I could contribute little to the subject, had given me the opportunity to study the setting.

We were interrupted by a boy who arrived to say that Bill's boat had just come across the bay. Then he ran off to tell someone else for the event of an arrival created such interest that the pleasure of announcing it became a privilege.

Being anxious to get back to my camp to obtain the mail, I assumed that Pierre would wish to go also but he did not, stating that he would come later. As I left, however, Celine blandly presented me with a gunnysack containing twenty fish as though she delivered such a parcel every day at exactly the same hour.

I had started to walk along the beach path in front of the Indian houses from Pierre's which occupied almost the furthest position from the slough when a group of women, about to embark for the same destination, made room in their boat for me.

We had a merry voyage as there were five paddles in use which caused some confusion and laughter. I felt very satisfied with life, having derived confidence from my visit, and was quite certain that my affairs had come fully under control.

As we approached the shore, the mad cries of fighting dogs

reverberated from behind the warehouse, with answering shrieks from people who intuitively recognized that no ordinary conflict had started. We bent our paddle blades against the water until the canoe shot half its length upon the beach. At one glance as I jumped up the bank, I saw Bill's dogs tied under the cache. My dogs, then, were fighting it out.

As I ran, my sensations were the same as when I first experienced a mob gone crazy with hatred—pounding, kicking, so overcome with a desire to kill that any other living thing became an object on which to vent one's violence. By this time, the hundred dogs in the settlement were howling in barrages up to a mile away. With all their noise, the penetrating sound of broken gasps for air stood out, the impact of heavy bodies flung one upon the other, the sharp cries which issue only from the pain when teeth tear flesh. This then was a fight to the death. I knew, and all knew better than I.

When I passed the corner of the warehouse my feet stuck suddenly to the ground and I gazed upon a scene of paralyzing fury. Such a picture of animal ferocity I had only seen in calendars sent north by makers of guns and shells, an art of overstimulated imaginations now come to life in one mad minute. A great mass of fur and foaming mouths tearing and leaping without seeming to separate held me spellbound. Close by, tense, with a long club raised, a man agilely moved from point to point on the periphery of the fighting circle. His tensely drawn face was immobile except for the hawklike eyes which seemed to follow every move. When a dog broke loose he brought the club down over its head with as heavy a blow as

D

the short and swift speed of the action would permit. Once I thought he must have crushed the animal's skull but it only shivered a moment from the concussion and in less than the time necessary for the second stroke had sprung back into the pile.

When I moved in to assist, the man turned me back sharply with hardly a word. Immediately I had interpreted the expression on his face. It told me, "These dogs will kill you quicker than themselves. I have all the trouble I can handle right now without taking care of you." I knew he was right and felt ashamed for that split second until I caught a slight smile from his eyes as I moved back which said "You may be ignorant but you are not a fool."

The snarling pack swerved from place to place. Then one dog broke loose, the others following hard on his tail for a few yards, only to stop as though overwhelmed by complete self-consciousness and guilt. The runaway had fallen, wriggling over the ground in a half-conscious effort to escape, dragging his rear legs and a lengthening trail of intestines behind him. When we walked up to him, he was already dead, his muscles jerking in the last stiffening of his torn body. His face dripped with the blood of the victors and his mouth was matted with hair. That was the end of Curly.

The other dogs walked off slowly licking their wounds. There was no use to bother with them; they would fight no more that day.

I walked back to my tent in a daze. Shortly afterwards Bill came over and said, "Well you lost a dog, but don't ever mix in a fight like that until you know what you're doing. They'll kill you if they ever get you on the ground. You will think they're friendly but when they get fresh blood in their mouths, they're like wolves."

He chuckled a little to make light of the matter, rolling himself a cigarette.

"Well, boy, how do you like the country?" he queried, not waiting for an answer. "Great place, Bear Lake. Everybody's crazy—if they weren't crazy, they wouldn't come here." His eyes were full of smiles radiating outwards through crow foot valleys to his cheeks.

I lit a fire and he went off to find a packet of letters which he had brought up from the Mackenzie. Loading the stove, I closed the draft, and went to look for my dogs. They were lying in their usual places, all licking themselves but Peter who had escaped unscathed. He acted guiltier than the rest, perhaps because he had a conscience, but only Scotty would look at me and he furtively, giving the slightest movement to his tail. Ginger had been hurt badly enough to suffer but Whitey was disdainful and still tired. I fastened the chains around their necks deep into their heavy fur. Somehow I was losing consideration for the minor comforts of living. We could be friends perhaps but there was a difference. I still hated to kill.

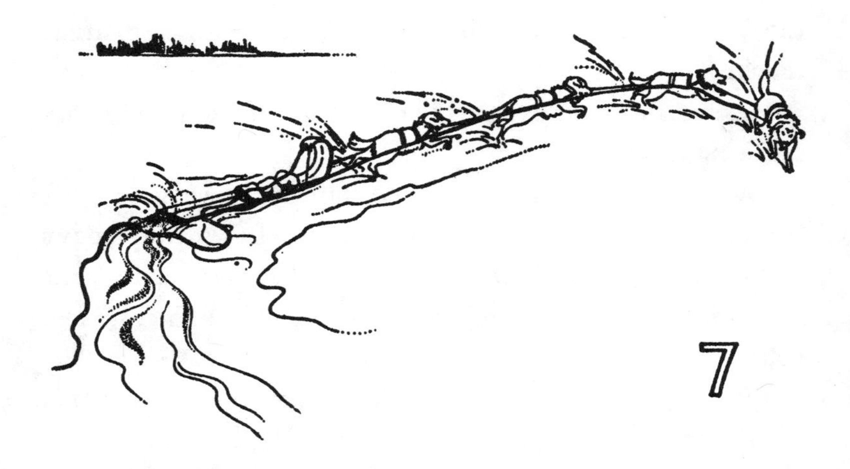

7

FISHING occupied the larger part of my time until I learned to avoid most of the complications which harry the novitiate. I had been warned to pile up wood and to saw it before the weather turned really cold. To do this, however, required searching some distance into the timber, as the nearer terrain had already been cleared of suitable trees. For several afternoons I had trudged off on unfamiliar snowshoes into the bush where I had found a stand of small dead spruce, the bark already beginning to peel from the desiccated trunks.

Stamping my snowshoes into a firm foundation, I hacked away easily in my shirt sleeves, pleasantly warm, despite the freezing air. When a tree crashed, however, my troubles began. Half the branches buried themselves in the snow which had been falling at intervals during the past weeks and when

I tried to approach to trim them off, they snagged the tips of my snowshoes, tumbling me into a tickling mass of needles. It struck me funny at first but after I had ripped the lacings of one shoe and soaked my mittens from filling them with snow, my temper rose. Even in October, wet mittens leave the hands stinging and it becomes necessary to dry them to avoid frostbite.

I came home faced with the problem of bringing in the dozen logs I had finally accumulated, and I decided to hitch up my toboggan in order to haul them. Once resolved on this course of action, I realized that I had been avoiding a challenge, a competition with my dogs to determine who would make decisions among us. Ever since the death of Curly they had been fighting among themselves, with bitter resentment for the restraint of chains.

I pulled my toboggan down from the roof of the store where it had been placed for protection. Its construction consisted of two oak boards, each the width I could spread my thumb and first finger, bent up into a flattened half circle, thirty inches high at the front with two wire stays leading down which, together with wood crosspieces, held the boards in position. Somehow it had an almost racy appearance since the forward fifth of its total ten-foot length narrowed to almost half its normal width. Along both sides, with intermittent fastenings, lay ropes to which one lashed the load. Most important for the driver, to the top of the curled fore part, through a hole in each of the pair of boards, was spliced the end of a four-fathom manila rope called the headline.

The harness, also imported into the country, hung from a crossbeam of the cache. For each dog there was a stuffed circular leather collar, just large enough to squeeze over the animal's head. Each side of the collar held a neck strap which joined the ends of a pair of backstraps, themselves to be fastened around the dog by snapping the bellyband. A pair of traces, buckled to the principal junction of the other straps, served to connect all the dogs in tandem to the toboggan.

When I dragged all this equipment over near the dogs, they became insane with the hope of moving. I laid out the harness, snapping the ends of the traces around the front loops of the side ropes of the toboggan. Unhooking Ginger's chain at the post, I tried to lead him to harness but he jumped into the air, almost pulling me off my feet. Then he ran dragging me along until I finally sat down to hold him. The near crazy beast relaxed somewhat but every time we started again he wanted to investigate in some new direction. Finally, almost exhausted from the effort, I brought him back to his stake.

All during this performance the dogs had been barking as loudly as possible and even Peter evinced more interest than he had ever shown before. I just watched them until they quieted down again.

For my next attempt, I unhooked the traces, leaving harness for only one dog. Into this I put Peter who behaved perfectly and I climbed aboard, excited in anticipation of a ride. Peter dashed off when commanded but as soon as we passed the edge of the tramped-down snow around the camp, my weight became too much for him and I had to run behind hanging onto the headline until we reached wind-swept areas where the snow had not accumulated sufficiently to break his stride.

The experience elated me and Peter's extraordinary response to my instructions restored my confidence completely. This playing, however, simply wasted my time, and I was aware that we should be working, so we returned to the tent and I reassembled the harness, leaving Peter in the lead. Then I brought Whitey into position behind him, having some difficulty pushing the collar over his head. He did not seem to mind and after I snapped his bellyband, he sat docilely on his haunches copying Peter. I concluded that my major mistake had been in choosing Ginger first.

Putting Scotty into harness offered no complications beyond his trying to lick my face each time my head came close to him and when I told him to sit down like the others he obeyed. Ginger retained some excitability but I threatened him with the end of the chain which chilled his ardor.

When all were ready, I stood on the back of the toboggan and grasped the headline firmly with both hands, the proper position I had been told for starting off. What happened after I yelled "All right," I did not discover for several seconds as my feet shot out from under me and I landed flat on my back in the snow.

By the time I had picked myself up the dogs were several hundred feet out in the muskeg, snarled in the brush of a snowdrift with my toboggan turned over on top of them. I walked after the team more surprised than annoyed. Scotty was panting from his sudden exertion while Whitey and

Ginger growled at each other. I cracked the caribou-skin whip that had been looped around my neck, silencing the dogs. Straightening the toboggan, I then pulled Peter by the collar until the line formed again. Peter looked at me in utter disgust, and said, just as plainly as if he had words, "If you don't know what you are doing, at least I wish you would please stop making a fool out of me." I told him I was sorry and I did feel somewhat ashamed of myself.

I tried to lead Peter into a clearing but as soon as we started to move the other dogs wanted to pass us, soon weaving the traces into cross patterns. There was no solution but to walk them home where I took the precaution of tying the headline to a heavy log. Straightening the traces obliged me to unharness all the dogs save Peter who was willing to roll over a few times, but not without evincing further contempt for what to him stood out as the limit in ridiculous performances. I tried to explain how I felt about the whole affair but he merely belched at the conclusion of my attempt.

When all had once more been readied, I pointed the team in the direction of the trail I had broken out to my wood cutting, loosened the headline, and lay flat on the toboggan clinging to the side ropes. At the signal, we shot out toward the timber, the toboggan swinging sidewise at every slight curve sending up a spray of snow into the air and almost carrying Ginger off his feet from the backlash of the load.

Just as I began to be enthusiastic over this wonderful experience of speeding over the country, the dogs stopped abruptly, letting the toboggan carry forward in its momentum, knocking Ginger on top of Scotty and frightening Whitey who had begun to urinate. Peter let out a single yelp which was clearly an oath. I pulled the toboggan backwards which resolved the trouble and after due delay we started off again on Peter's volition, Ginger turning his head in startled protest as he hopped along on three legs, still squirting away.

We had turned off into a flat area of drifted snow over which Peter had decided the running was easier. Our speed had abated and although I enjoyed the ride, I discovered that the enterprise had exhausted me. Before long, again we stopped and Ginger stepped off the trail to defecate. His delicacy in pulling over astounded me but we had not gone far before each of the other dogs did exactly the same.

Our reduced speed, together with so much starting and stopping gave me confidence and I stood up on the toboggan to locate our position. Peter had made a wide loop in the open flats so that we were now facing our camp about a half mile away. Apparently as I discovered this, the dogs did also and they leapt forward toward home, once again tossing me upside down. When I cleared my eyes, the dogs were racing at full speed across the muskeg with the headline snaking out behind the empty sleigh.

There was no choice but to plow through the snow after them, which, since I was already weary, made a depressing finale to my first trip by dog team. As I came near the buildings I noticed a group of people leaning against the walls or sitting on convenient logs. Bill was there with his whole family as well as a dozen other Indians. It suddenly struck me from their postures that they had been watching a show for some time. Peter, I thought, knew all along.

My face flushed as I walked by, suddenly mad and swearing under my breath. The team had overshot the camp in their speed and were fouled around a cache post. I led the dogs back to their stakes and unharnessed them while the Indians shuffled off in groups, still silent except for some of the children. Bill, as he passed by yelled at me and I could make out the friendliness in his eyes.

"You're doing all right, boy. Better try using only three dogs for a while," and he continued on down to the slough.

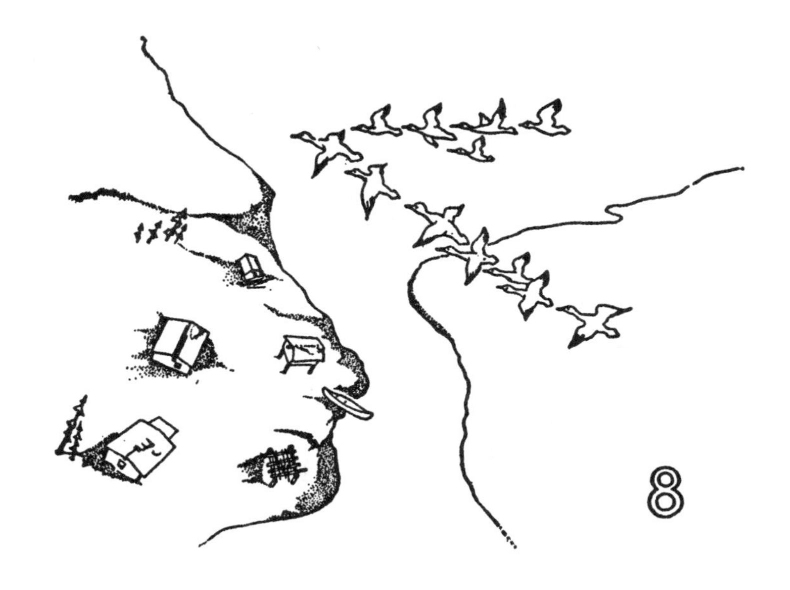

8

SHORTLY after I had unhitched my team following our first brief but exciting trip together, Bill's son appeared with an invitation from his father to have supper at their house. This in all probability meant not only an excellent meal but the opportunity to learn more about dogs from a man who, among trappers and adventurers living alone in the north, had gained such admiration for a perfect adaptation to the country that his name was quietly mentioned with respect throughout the whole Mackenzie region.

The house which he had built some ten years previously from logs squared with a broadax was roughly twenty-five feet on a side. It had a low gabled roof covered with earth from which patches of dry grass still stood up where heat from the interior had melted the snow.

On entering one came into a long room comprising the larger part of the building, the remainder being divided to serve as two bedrooms. The appearance struck me as dun-colored and drab, with a gray quality emphasized by the limited illumination supplied by candles. For a few minutes I could see little, but after sitting down at a narrow table along one side of the main room, my eyes became accustomed to the murkiness and I made out women and children hugging the darker peripheries between various pieces of rough furniture accommodating the appurtenances of family life. The almost unique article among all else was a standard cast-iron kitchen stove, a luxury seldom seen in such isolated communities where cakes and pies represent forgotten or perhaps unknown and consequently unwanted symbols of civilization.

Nothing passed by the sensitivity of my host who said with a wry smile, almost answering my half-conscious uncertainties, "Not much to look at, but you'll be glad to see the light in the window before the winter is over."

He pushed a can of silk cut tobacco toward me and cigarette papers from which he had just previously helped himself. He was a spare man of medium height in his late thirties, with graying hair which had receded noticeably over his forehead. Of his costume itself there was nothing remarkable unless one noticed his pants. The rubbers over mooseskin moccasins and the dark-blue button-up sweater comprised standard cover for men at home in the settlement but the pants had a character of their own. They were striped morning trousers of a fine heavy cloth which looked as though they had been worn continuously for years. Also they were too large around the waist leaving folds that drooped along the thighs in a pattern so old as to have gained immunity from any casual creasing. Somehow they epitomized the disregard of self-interest for which he was reputed.

The dinner consisted principally of ducks which my host had shot at the edge of the lake that morning.

"There won't be many more this fall," he said, "but boy, you'll think them a pretty sight when they fly back in the spring!"

For me, spring seemed so far off, it failed of having reality but I asked, letting my thoughts drift from the word, whether that time of year was pleasant on the Lake.

His eyes sparkled as he answered. "People say of the Lake that we have only two seasons here—winter and August. In July you can still travel on the ice with dogs, and before September is over the country is covered with snow. Just the same, when the long days come again and the temperature goes up to twenty below, you'll think it's spring."

A little shudder rippled across my back but I laughed with him for his own complete lack of fear outweighed my insecurity.

"Winter is like a woman," he continued, "you will love and you will hate her, but once you've lived with her you'll never leave. We all say we are going out to civilization and never come back again. It does no good. One summer outside and we hit for the River and down we come. It snows and there she is, lying there stretched out white and beautiful under the arctic moon. Then we start cursing her all over again. You will see. Have a smoke?"

We had finished our dinner and moved across the room to make space at the table for the younger children to eat while the women cleaned up the dishes with a homely clatter. I began to ask questions about the myriad things necessary for me to learn. It was then that I discovered the rarest quality about the man. His cynical humor disappeared abruptly and he started to explain what I wanted to know, moving from point to point with such careful consideration for my understanding, that I had the impression of memorizing a medical prescription in which the slightest error would change the result from life to death. Nor was the formula simple, but rather one which demanded judgment in the mixing. Each move had to be evaluated from many points of view, often uncertain and requiring elaborations which compounded data of varying degrees of validity. Never before had I encountered such precision or accuracy in the exposition of human experience.

His black eyes reflected the flickering candlelight while the end of his long and slightly drooping nose moved sensitively in coordination with his mouth. Except for that element intrinsic in the modulation of a voice, he talked without emotion like one obviously catalyzed by the controlled processes of his reasoning.

The evening wore on well toward morning and our conversation lightened over cups of hot cocoa. I was reviewing my sensations during the afternoon's ride and mentioned that the dogs stopped and stepped aside to relieve themselves.

"The dogs are taught to do that," he explained, "otherwise fresh excrement on the trail would stick to the bottom of the toboggan, freeze, and make it hard to pull."

The reason, once given, was so obvious I felt stupid. While we were talking, my dogs commenced to bark angrily at each other and a look of annoyance crossed my companion's face. "They will never keep quiet until there is a new boss of the team."

His remark made me flush and he hastened to add, "Not you—another dog." Seeing that I did not comprehend him he went on. "In every team there is one dog which dominates the others. If there is a fight, he pitches in and breaks it up. After the rest have been licked sufficiently, generally a few growls will stop the trouble before it starts. Curly was the boss of your outfit and now that big sandy fellow wants to scrap it out with the white one."

"Is that bad?"

"Not so bad here," he laughed, "except for the noise. If it happened on the trail a long way from home, that might be serious."

I did not see the reason and he explained.

"Supposing you are off some place in the bush where you are depending on those dogs to pull a heavy load and then one night they get into a fight and kill or cripple each other."

"I get the point," I interrupted.

"Besides," he went on, "those dogs of yours are worth a lot

of money. A trapper on the Mackenzie offered five hundred dollars for old Pete last winter. There isn't another leader like him in the whole country. Why that damn dog can almost write his own name. Every time an Indian has showed up in the store this year, the first thing he wants is to see that dog of yours."

"Isn't your leader just as good?"

Bill laughed. "That's different. I wouldn't sell Spot for a thousand dollars but I've had him for almost ten years. He's getting a little old, poor fellow, but—well you'll know what I mean before you're through."

"Peter doesn't look very big," I countered, having admired Spot for his solid hundred pounds of muscle.

"You're right, Pete is not a big dog but he has brains and knows how to use them as you will probably learn. They tell me an old miner near Kotzebue in Alaska raised him as a pet. Pete has already traveled halfway across the arctic and I wouldn't be surprised, providing you could make him understand that you wanted him to go back, that he'd find his way alone."

"Have you noticed when he is hitched up that you have to say 'All right!' to make him move? Everyone else says *marche'* around here and when someone yells it, all the dogs rush off. Pete pays no attention to anyone. The man who taught him must have worked with horses once because Pete also answers only to 'gee' and 'haw' while the people in this country use the expressions 'hew' and 'chaw' to signal a turn to right and left. Most of the time, their dogs pay no attention to them anyway."

The tribute to Peter made me very proud and I thus became aware of a new status in the community as the owner of the best lead dog. Avid for more knowledge, if not praise of the team, I asked about the others in it.

"There isn't a poor dog in the lot. The black and white one is perhaps a little fast for the others and pulls harder. The young one you call Ginger possibly isn't up to the rest but he is said to be a smart steer dog."

"You mean a leader, like Pete?"

"No, a steer or wheel dog hitched nearest the toboggan.

My ignorance manifested itself in my face so Bill went on to describe the functions incumbent upon that position.

"When you drive a string of dogs along a trail through the bush, your road frequently twists because of trees or other obstructions. When all the dogs are running fast and you turn sharply, the strain on the traces naturally tends to pull the front of the toboggan sidewise. Then it may crash against a tree and split the headboards or at least break the harness. The steer dog next to the sleigh prevents this by immediately leading off at a sixty-degree angle from the direction the others are going, thereby compensating for the sidewise stress and keeping the toboggan in the clear until the bend has been passed."

This matter explained I felt suddenly weary, not only from so much new knowledge, but out of realization of what must yet be experienced. Bill was tired himself and I interpreted his reaction as partly a response to an unpromising pupil.

We bade each other goodnight rather abruptly and I walked back to my tent, first stopping to look at my dogs. They all lay curled in the snow but Ginger raised his head slightly to glance at me over his shoulder.

"So you are a steer dog," I said.

9

PIERRE woke me in the morning, pushing into the tent unabashed and saying "Jees Chris', ees thees where you are livin'? I bro't you a bag of feesh."

He pulled off his mittens and laid the fire with the shavings I had already cut as a helpful preparation for unusually cool or discouraging mornings. This day promised to be a good one, however, for the thermometer read in the high twenties and Pierre's arrival with the fish had cheered me. Despite the number of people around the camp my total conversations had amounted to only a few hours during the past weeks and I hungered to talk with someone.

Pierre stood up, bumping the tent wall, and he twisted aside almost losing his balance from surprise.

"Goddam," he ejaculated, "thees place would be all right for a beaver or to crawl in weeth a wooman, maybe." Then he laughed like rippling water in a mountain brook. His humor was contagious irrespective of the words which he had not offered as funny although he punctuated his sentences with chuckles.

"We'll fix your net first and then hunt duck, yes?"

His remark came out more as a simple statement than a question and he began to rummage in my grub box for the tea. I was discovering that nothing could be too urgent to interfere with a preliminary cup of bitter brew.

The fishing had been poor because of storms which had apparently driven the schools offshore. Once a blizzard stopped the visiting and on the last opportunity to go out I had taken only forty. The dilemma had been the same for almost all, but an Indian had said that late one night Celine had emptied her nets all alone.

Bill had cautioned me that there would be a diminishing number of fish until after freeze-up but that if I could tide myself over that period I should find plenty later on, especially from December through February when there would be no limit to the potential catch. My second net had been prepared and while I dressed and hunted out a box of cartridges, we drank our tea.

With the canoe loaded, Pierre directed me into the bow. "You seet there," he said. "I don't want that you mistake me for a duck."

His direction was wholly gratuitous but he could not forego

the opportunity for the comment, probably born of some reasonable uncertainty as to my experience as a hunter.

We paddled out into the bay to set the net but Pierre could not make up his mind which location would be the most favorable. He irritated me with his unmistakable rationalizations in choosing a place, argument so voluble as to preclude any thinking he might have given to the matter. Finally he agreed to feed the net out just beyond my first one.

All went well until the last anchor stone went overboard, somehow tangling the fastening to the buoy and dragging that entire end to the bottom. Pierre laughed but I became infuriated. Then he said, "We let Celine fix," and shrugged his shoulders, still laughing. This made me hilarious as I realized that both of us had been thinking exactly that for the past half hour.

We stopped to visit the other net but found only seventeen fish, all in the end opposite to the one we had just dropped. By that time, however, the sunshine had made us gay and we were beyond concern over the food supply.

We paddled back through the slough and down along the shore of the little lake where the sedges, still washed free of ice, rippled in the breeze. Coming around a tiny point, we flushed three white-winged scoters a few yards away. With the first barrel, I caught two that never had a chance to get into the air but missed the third, the shot spattering the water in its wake. Several others flew from cover near the end of the lake and we concluded our hunting had ended for a while. Pierre picked up the dead duck and then stopped the other with a paddle where it feebly struggled to swim away.

"Celine will cook very good. You can come and eat with us," invited Pierre.

We moved on quietly up the pond toward the narrowed end near the mouth of its tributary stream, there letting the canoe lie lazily up against a drift log. Our discussion had turned from fish to ducks and then to women. Pierre told me of his boyhood in Quebec and how year after year he had trapped farther north until he reached the lower Mackenzie. His tales of Indian girls held all the spice and frankness of unrestrained Gallic culture but withal such warmth and human sympathy that his loves took on a richer quality than might be expected of an ordinary man's recounting. He seemed compelled by some inner urge to justify his marriage, and insisted that no one could expect a native bride to be a virgin. He had been certain soon after he had met Celine at her father's hunting camp that she was going to be his woman. What difference did it make if she had previously lived with a man, he argued. In that respect, he viewed all females as alike.

Not to seem unappreciative of his frankness, I told him of a girl I had known in Paris. Perhaps the quiet setting of the lake in the shadow of the hills loosened the flow of words from my heart for I related my story with intense feeling, lyrically compressed from the loneliness which his own confidence had instilled.

When I was finished he said, "There are many woman who people say are bad because they live with men but they are sometimes wrong." He had suddenly begun to tremble and tears rolled down from his eyes. "The're bastards, thos' dirty people. I have live with many good woman who make their life that way."

His enthusiasm was rising rapidly. "Yes sir, I tell you, whores ees one of the bes' goddam kind of peoples in the whole worl'!"

Then we both laughed so loud that small animals scurried along the bank a hundred feet away.

We sat and looked out over the water while Pierre sang "Sous le pont de Paris." A muskrat swam along the shore leaving a tiny ripple behind him as he hurried off.

"I call him. You shoot him!" said Pierre.

"What's the joke now," I gibed.

The idea of calling muskrats struck me as one more of Pierre's exaggerations but he insisted that he could make the same whistling sounds that muskrats use themselves. He demonstrated a series of sibilants induced by sucking in air between his nearly closed lips, the result being not unlike the chatter of a squirrel only more drawn out and less iterative. I tried to copy him but despite his encouragements, the results did not suit me. He continued, preoccupied by his accomplishment.

As I rested from my efforts, I noticed a muskrat making his way in our general direction. When Pierre discovered my fascinated stare, he too saw the muskrat and intensified his chirping, giving to it an almost plaintive quality.

The animal clearly shifted its course and swam directly toward us as though Pierre suddenly had become invested with supernatural powers.

"Shoot it, shoot it!" he yelled, causing the swimmer to shift its course instantly and make for the sedgy shore.

Unprepared as I was, I hit the little beast just as it was about to escape from view. Pierre paddled over and took the animal aboard. Its bedraggled wet body showed little resemblance to the prime fur with which women warm themselves.

I asked what he thought he would do with it and he suggested that we might eat it. Amused, I wanted him to describe how to cook muskrat and he explained that the procedure required no more than skinning off the pelt and boiling the carcass in water, first tying the tail to the handle of the kettle. This detail made me dubious but Pierre assured me with all seriousness that muskrat meat tasted fine and that he had seen natives tie the tails so that the rats could be pulled out of boiling water the more easily.

All the way home, Pierre continued to elaborate on the tastiness of boiled muskrat and on the widespread appreciation of this dish. He seemed almost hurt at my obvious restraint in accepting his account in its entirety. Finally just before we landed, I said, "Okay, Pierre, let's eat it."

He thought I was joking but I convinced him that a little muskrat appealed to me as a change from my fish diet. Finally he said, "Muskrats don't taste good unless they're fat. I think we wait till spring."

10

A BLIZZARD through the day and night had laid a heavy covering over the land, creating a scene of simple contrasts between the clean snow and the blue water with its reflecting sky. I was searching out some poles for firewood which had been lost from sight when I heard Bill at the edge of the slough yell for me to bring my shotgun. Picking it up, I ran down anticipating the pleasure of eating more ducks.

As I approached him he pointed to the high cache where a white owl rested at the end of the ridgepole. The bird charmed me, as it seemed somehow to give life to the landscape with a particular appropriateness, even as does an albatross in the southern ocean. Suddenly the bird flew away with a flutter of wings, dipping over the house and disappearing toward the timber.

Bill wanted to know why I did not shoot it. My gun had remained forgotten in my hands and there had been no desire to kill the owl. There was something in me that resented the Indian habit of firing at everything in sight. For myself, I had to suppress my emotions before I could destroy the strange and the beautiful.

I told Bill that never having seen that species of bird before, I had been distracted and considered it obviously of no advantage to have the bird dead anyway.

Bill smiled a little paternally. "Maybe so, boy, but I'd say you have lost a chance for the best meal you will ever eat in the north."

This surprised me but I did not doubt him as I had learned that Bill seldom made an error of judgment concerning anything which belonged to his isolated environment.

We walked back to the tent and he sat down on the chopping block, surveying the camp while I replaced the gun.

"You will not find living in such cramped quarters all winter very comfortable," he said slowly. "A silk tent has the advantage of being easy to carry but you may burn it down using that tin stove. I have been thinking that perhaps you could fix up the little cabin down at the end of the slough. It has been housing the dogs but by this time perhaps that won't bother you."

He smiled at the enthusiasm of my answer, "Hell, no! It would be perfect for me if it's all right with you."

"You had better take a look at it first. It's not much of a shack," he responded.

I had moved in from the moment of his suggestion and already had visions of how I would adapt it to my comfort.

We walked down past his cache. The shack did diminish somewhat in size as I looked at it from close range but Bill, who as usual sensed my thoughts said with a twinkle in his eyes, "Anyway, you won't have too much wood to cut in order to heat it."

This was a happy thought for the acquisition of my winter's fuel supply still remained ahead of me, another task in which I had fallen behind the economical schedule of preparations.

"I wonder how big it actually is?" My emphasis had returned to enthusiasm.

"If you really want to know, we can find that out," he answered, ambling off to his store.

I walked around the building looking at it from all sides until he returned with a battered rule.

We opened the door and bending low stepped over the uncut bottom log. The interior was musty and partly filled with snow which had blown in through chinks between the wall logs. The main deficiencies lay in the space cut for a window, open without a frame, and in the lack of any floor but the natural dirt which unfortunately contained several protruding boulders of considerable size.

"I think I have a window sash somewhere," said Bill, sizing up the situation, "but for God's sake don't break it or you will have to walk a thousand miles to find another. As for the rocks, I guess your back is pretty strong," and he nudged me playfully.

I took the ruler and began to measure. From front to rear the cabin was thirteen feet, but the width was only eight feet seven inches. It would be best I decided to build a bunk across the back, diagonally placed with reference to the little door which extended only four feet high and less than two feet wide. Fortunately, the shack had been constructed high enough to enable one to stand upright for the ridgepole, a good half foot in diameter, rested two inches short of eight feet above what I judged to be the average level of the floor.

The roof with its corrugated under surface comprised forty-four closely placed spruce poles on each slope, covered with sods and extending from the ridge to the top of the eleven logs which made up the five-foot side walls. The sodding had deteriorated for I could make out bits of blue sky at frequent intervals. Since there would be no more rain until spring, I liked the idea of a starlight roof but Bill warned me that I would prefer to have the shack warm and do my stargazing outside.

In the middle of the west wall, to the left of the door as one entered, four of the upper logs had been cut to leave an aperture about two feet square for a window. Under this I contemplated building a table, still allowing between it and the front end of the cabin enough room for the stove.

"Let's see what we can find to help you fix it up," suggested Bill, turning sidewise to duck through the door.

Happy over things to come, I followed him. He stopped

for a minute to make a quick estimate of the outside of the house.

"You will certainly have to mud those walls," he said, laughing softly. When I asked why he was amused, he explained that daubing wet dirt into chinks, a task which could only be done successfully in freezing weather, could hardly be considered a pleasant undertaking by anyone. I was beyond discouragement, however, and gaily walked up to the dilapidated building which served him as a combination store and warehouse.

He unlocked the door and we stepped into the murky interior illuminated by one front window. It was like moving back a century into the time of the *coureurs de bois* for the difference between this and the white painted trading rooms of the Hudson's Bay Company "forts" represented the extreme limits of contrast which had developed in the fur trade. Independent traders on the River who used their homes in which to buy and sell, or stores hidden away in the Kentucky hills, have an unavoidably modern character compared to Bill's outpost at the edge of the Barrens.

Moving around was like working oneself through a heavy undergrowth of willows at the edge of a river. Hanging from the ceiling were bunches of traps, coils of rope, a few women's and children's dresses, drooping shanks of binding twine, half-moldy bearskins, besides numerous other objects unrecognizable to me, almost all of which gave the impression of having been untouched for years, as though left by some long-dead merchant. Boxes stood up here and there on the floor like stumps in a clearing, each more or less open according to the requirements of removing its contents, which if not too large left table space for bolts of cottonade and striped or fancy flannelette.

Two of the walls were as crowded as the ceiling or the floor. Dog chains hung next to stovepipe elbows and a few tweed caps, apparently an odd acquisition, bunched out above a water bucket. The front wall with its window remained clear except for a few washbasins and strange bits of things, hung on nails to free the owner's hands when he entered. One could reconstruct elements of history from those pieces. In my imagination I wrote, "The trader was mending his dog harness when Susi Big-water wanted 'to see store'," and things of that sort. Bill translated the Indian expression "to see store" literally, as it struck him funny, but I did not ask whether it was for the same reason which seemed apt to me.

In front of the remaining wall stood a homemade counter, with a small glass cabinet at the end. These comprised the only objects in the room, except the stove adapted from a fifty-gallon gasoline drum, which could be called furniture. On the counter, I noticed a partly emptied box of eight-inch candles, an article of which I was in need, so I asked the price.

"They sell two for a quarter but I'll charge you only twenty-five percent on the cost landed. There aren't enough to last long so you had better take all you want."

I did not know how many, so he gave me one of his few

boxes with the comment that he would be glad to take back any that I did not use.

This transaction typified the man whose generosity embarrassed me in a country where prices were often astronomical. I knew that his profits by selling for fur would have multiplied any he made from me.

Behind the counter rose a series of shelves containing tea, matches, tobacco, cartridges, and a variety of similar articles. While he was searching in the corners for some object, I noted that the little glass cabinet held smaller items, some for the luxury trade. A few assorted pocketknives, a pipe with a shiny synthetic stem, two or three pairs of metal snowglasses, besides miscellaneous pins and needles had been piled up on top of each other.

Bill came out between a pile of women's fleece-lined drawers and a keg of spikes, trailing a heavy steel pry bar.

"I knew it was around somewhere. You'd never get those rocks out of the floor without it. Now for the window."

Taking a lighted candle we went into the storeroom, an eight-by-twelve lean-to which had been added to the side of the building. The area was crowded with boxes also, but unopened and with an overflow of hundred-pound bags of flour piled on top for which there had been no more room in the high cache. Above the only passageway hung bunches of fur, mostly lynx and foxes but a few marten and mink besides. The tails brushed my face as I moved behind them, leaving with me the pungent musky smell of untanned pelts.

"Mark that fur," said Bill, handing me the candle, "or you will singe it!"

Bill tugged away at a few boxes and finally passed over the top to me a glazed window frame. I thought he was through but he kept on until he finally uncovered a small cast-iron stove.

"Here's something. The first stove I ever brought up to the Lake." His face took on the smile of pleasant memories. "I've warmed my feet near that one many a time."

We carried the things into the store and put them down.

"Better leave them here until you get the rough work finished. Somewhere, I should be able to find the old drum oven that went with this rig. Boy, you're going to be all fixed up!"

11

PRYING up the boulders from the floor of my cabin proved to be a more arduous undertaking than I had anticipated. Some stones, which interfered but slightly with the even surface that I demanded, developed into mammoth proportions as they became exposed. These I levered to one side to wait assistance for I could not lift them over the six-inch doorsill of my house.

By the second day of my efforts, I decided that the ideal had been achieved, adding a little more headroom for my comfort. Both because I had burned up all my firewood and needed poles with which to construct a bed, I decided to hitch up the dogs and bring back a supply from my cutting beyond the muskeg.

Following Bill's advice, I unbuckled the harness for one dog and proceeded to fasten Peter, Whitey, and Scotty to the toboggan. Ginger became furious because he was left chained, jumping up and down, fairly screeching, as his leash stifled the cries in his throat. It gained him nothing for we set off without him, I having secured myself for the start.

After the customary stops, for which I had learned to drag my foot as a brake, we moved along briskly. Peter broke trail easily through the snow which the midday sun had thickened into a solid footing as far as the edge of the timber. At that point, I went ahead on my snowshoes, leading the way up the hill, for I was somewhat uncertain of our route, the recent white blanket having weighed down the spruce branches, transforming the whole forest into an unrecognizable fairyland.

Since I had piled my logs around my cutting, the spot was easily located from the fresh stumps. I turned the team about, settling the toboggan on a level space and heaved the logs onto it, a medium-sized one in the middle and the two largest on the outside, their butts in the opposite direction to the first. Then I added two more on top.

This done, I set out to cut some poles for my bed, a task I accomplished with ease as I needed only small green spruce trees which grew plentifully near by. Having trimmed a dozen, I piled them around the logs, making quite a bulky load when laced over by looping a line under the side ropes of the toboggan.

On saying "All right!" to Peter, the dogs started with a rush, rapidly gaining speed down the slope. I had already projected my next activities at home when the top-heavy toboggan careened over on its side, jerking the whole team off its feet. Each of the three dogs turned and looked at me with exactly the same exasperated expression as though they were saying, "Now you have done it again."

Instead of feeling sorry, I chided them for going so fast. The situation did not seem one to worry about and I told Peter not to be such an old soreface, but he just looked at me as if he thought it was impossible for anyone to be so stupid; then he licked his jowls and apparently settled down for a long stay.

I maneuvered my snowshoes around to the middle of the lower side of the toboggan and leaned heavily against the top logs to push them right side up but they did not budge. I braced myself more squarely and pressed my whole weight against the load, but I would have had equal success if I had tried to shift the entire hill.

Peter stared at me like a professor gazing at a hopeless student over his spectacles. "Why God damn you!" I said, hating him for his irritating superiority. He lowered his eyes and cautiously put his head between his paws.

To repair the situation required the complete unloading of the toboggan, setting it straight again, and once more restoring the logs to their proper position. This demanded many times the energy given to the original undertaking for the heavy pieces, now twisted, had jammed the lashing unreachably underneath the pile. After straining for what seemed an interminable time, I loosened some of the poles by pulling them out rearwards, thus freeing the pressure. Then, since no flat place was accessible, the toboggan had to be reloaded on a slant, during which business one of the tree trunks rolled off smashing the front of a snowshoe, leaving it a flabby crumpled snarl of woven sinew than which nothing looks more symbolically disastrous in relation to the insignificance of the damage.

When ready to move again, I looped the end of the headline around the middle of the load, and straining on it from the upper side, thus eased the team down the hill, making a precautionary halt every few yards. In this way we arrived at the flats, having taken more than an hour to travel the quarter of a mile.

For safety's sake as well as some concern for appearance, I straightened up the load which had no parts remaining parallel. Then I climbed on top and we sped along the trail riding smoothly like a ship in full ballast. The wind cooled me and my mind relaxed as I listened to the rhythmical patter of homeward-beating feet.

I stacked the heavy logs about ten feet in front of the door where they would act as a snowbreak and at the same time be convenient for sawing. Making a bunk, surprisingly enough, gave me less trouble than I expected, once I had obtained a score of spikes from Bill. Burying a vertical post in the floor and nailing it to the roof took the longest time. Then sharpening a pole with a length equal to a little more than the width of my shoulders, I drove it between two wall logs at the end of the cabin and spiked the free end to the vertical post a little over knee height above the floor. Taking nine of my poles, I cut them into seven-foot lengths, sharpening the butts of every other one and the tips of the remainder. The prepared ends fitted between two side-wall logs and rested over the top of my previously placed horizontal. To be safe, I nailed a support under them at the wall and, after removing the long poles, wedged in another horizontal piece for the middle, supporting the free end of the latter on a section of log which I had intended splitting for firewood. When I had knocked in the nine poles side by side and driven a nail through each, the bed needed only a mattress of spruce boughs.

I was gazing with satisfaction at the result when Pierre stuck his head in the door.

"You got a new house, I see," he said, sniffling and smiling at the same time. "That's very good. We been afraid you burn up in that tent some night." He laughed as though the thought of anyone being really warm pleased him very much.

"Come on in and see how you like it."

"Jees Chris'," he ejaculated, stumbling over the doorsill, "thees house must been built for a bitch pup."

"Good—very good," he said looking around, "but that bed, she is too high for to be cool."

"Cool, hell," I answered. "With the roof I've got, I should sling a hammock from it to catch a little of the heat going out." My voice had a stolen ring of authority which made me realize that I had acquired a touch of sophistication in the ways of the country.

"Maybe you right—if you sleep alone," he said, twisting his neck to get various views through the ceiling and finally tripping over a boulder.

"That reminds me, Pierre, I hear that you are one of the strongest men ever to live at the Lake."

He understood immediately, looking first at me and then at the rocks.

"You can't lift him?"

"Not out the door."

He pulled his blanket parka over his head and rolled one of the biggest stones in front of the opening. Then he squatted down over it, wrapping his arms around its lower half. He grunted for a few seconds. I was about to help him when the boulder began to roll up and forward, moved as much by his chest, it would seem, as by the strength of his arms. With the rock a few inches off the floor he appeared to work himself under it. Then he was stopped. I tried to assist but he ordered me away gasping. His face had turned red and his forehead bubbled with perspiration. I began to be afraid, in part that he might injure himself, but more for what might happen if he failed. Living so much alone, I had become supersensitive to the feelings of those with whom I shared my rare contacts. At last, giving his final strength, he heaved the stone over the sill and fell on top of it.

I showed honest amazement at the strength of this wiry little man which seemed to facilitate his recovery.

"We be smart with the other ones," he said. He picked up a few leftover pole ends and built a ramp, using a section of log as underpinning. Together we pushed the other stones out and deposited them at the side of the cabin. The effort was tiring and we rested for a few minutes but my interest in finishing my house impelled me to work again. Pierre, having made his contribution, left, saying that he was going to hunt ptarmigan.

12

COMPLETING my house took longer than I expected, as I had to interrupt my efforts with such daily chores as splitting firewood, cooking, and finding food for the dogs. The supply of fish had fallen off and, although Celine had fixed my second net, we were catching but few more than our immediate needs demanded. The loss of Curly had reduced the requirements somewhat, and I fed the dogs only three fish each evening which, considering that they worked very little, were sufficient to keep them healthy. They would have liked more, however, but limited their reaction to staring at me with soft and appealing eyes. Since there was so much time to think, my mind periodically recreated their expression of longing to plague me, although I was only half conscious of annoyance, even as one becomes toward insects in the summer.

I had built a table twenty inches wide beneath the window, the top made from the fairly smooth boards of a large box given me by Bill together with the stove and old drum oven that he had found. He smothered his generosity by saying that I was improving his property so we let it go at that.

A couple of steel-strapped cases which had contained lump sugar served as stools and I was satisfied that my furnishings were completed except for a few shelves which I planned to install when the mood came upon me.

As Bill had prophesied, the most unpleasant job had been to dig clay along the lake bank and haul it back to the cabin; then, after watering it into a paste, to smear it over the moss between the logs. In the first place, the clay, which consisted mostly of dirt, almost paralyzed my hands as it froze. Working in ice water alone would not have been so painful for one could dry one's fingers quickly, but to attempt to do so when they were covered with clayey muck took so long that the whole bucket of paste solidified in the meantime. My solution was to keep an extra kettle of hot mixing water on the stove and when my hands became numb, I would thrust them into it. By the time I was finishing the fourth wall, I wished that I had never seen the shack. The task completed, however, I felt very much satisfied with the bands of shiny packing, frozen in gray stripes between all the logs. In truth, the clay was thin in spots, but from the inside one could not see any sunlight through the chinks.

The roof had not fared so well. It was too late in the season to cut sods successfully and I had spread only a light coat of dirt before a heavy blizzard put an end to my endeavors.

Sometimes for hours I would sit at my table and gaze through the little window at the snow, hypnotized by the incessant whiteness, dreaming of my past life and projecting fantasies of some future year. Out of abstract thoughts, I conjured physical women who excited my passions, until weary of the play I cast them aside to find myself trembling in the cold, the fire in my stove having long since burned out.

One afternoon, when I had befuddled myself with too much sitting, an Indian boy stopped with a note from Pierre announcing that his wife had killed a moose and asking me to come to dinner. The Indian ferried me across the slough and I walked along the well-broken trail through the settlement carrying in my hand a doubled dog chain. It had been a satisfaction to learn that by jingling it, I could turn back the occasional cur that might be loose, for the sound was associated in their minds with a fearful beating.

No dog did bother me but as I passed an open stretch near my destination I saw a woman whose age I guessed to be about thirty, lying beside one of the alternate paths and crying loudly. My first impulse moved me to offer aid but as I listened, I sensed her pain was not wholly physical, and that no harm would come from at least bringing the situation to Celine's attention before intruding.

When Pierre let me in, I pointed out the woman and he became quite excited, attacking Celine with the problem.

Celine, unmoved as usual, explained in short blunt statements that the woman's husband had just caught her in sexual intercourse with his cousin and had beaten her, but not severely. When I became curious over what further consequences might follow, Celine simply reported that the irate spouse had been telling everyone, "Just wait until my cousin gets a wife." Perhaps in part as an escape from anxiety in the matter, this made me laugh so hard that my hosts eyed each other in surprise.

Celine was baking a moose heart. Pierre reiterated the complaint that the fishing had been poor and added that the Indians were blaming the lack of food on Celine for having broken a taboo in visiting nets too soon after unsuccessfully giving birth to a child. This offended the fish, they said, causing them to swim into deeper water.

Celine, on the other hand, undisturbed in her earthy realism, had disregarded the gossip, and setting out early one morning, had shot a moose, tracks of which had been reported by two youths who had failed to approach it. She had cleaned the animal, bringing in several choice parts wrapped up in the skin. Several men had already left with toboggans to transport the remainder.

Pierre, proud of her accomplishment, elaborated on her abilities as a hunter, which I noted for the first time elicited a personal reaction from his wife who flushed slightly at the praise. Clearly she enjoyed the tribute and merely interrupted to clarify a point when her husband narrated the details. He told how, immediately after killing the moose, she had cut off its ears and thrown them up in a tree so, as she said, they would not hear her and warn other animals on the next occasion that she went hunting. Then she cut off the nose and cooked it.

I thought perhaps eating the nose prevented the animal from also smelling her but she interrupted to say that a moose has marvelous hearing and does not trust to its nose in detecting danger. Pierre went on to add that Celine considered moose nose as a special delicacy but to his taste, it had the flavor and texture of a worn rubber heel. We concluded the discussion by Celine's promising to save a piece of the next one for me. Whatever opinion could be held about the nose, the heart, dripping with gravy proved delectable, and I in my turn found Celine responsive to appreciation.

After supper, my hostess brought out a bundle wrapped like dirty laundry in a large cloth. She opened it perfunctorily and took out a new white blanket parka sewn so that the black band of the ends made a border around the skirt. All the edges had been trimmed with the fur of lynx paws. Delighted, I put it on and paraded around the room like a boy in his first man's suit. My pleasure expanded to include both the maker and her husband, who hastened to show me the Eskimo-style boots, two sets of duffel socks, and a pair of blanket-lined mooseskin mittens likewise trimmed with lynx paws and tied together with a soft skin band long enough to reach around the neck.

My gratification, both real and sustained, embarrassed them and after there was nothing more to say I was still so happy over my new winter costume that I could tolerate no other interest. Excusing myself, I put on the parka and mittens and set out for home.

At the slough, I was forced to yell for someone to ferry me across. I could see a light but time was consumed in attracting attention for since all the dogs knew me, they remained quiet. Finally Bill shuffled down to the bank and in a few strokes had accomplished the round trip.

He did not like to be disturbed, and because I knew it I had avoided walking to the Indian village when transportation by water was not available. My own canoe had been smashed in transport and, considering that the Lake would soon be frozen, I had been advised against replacing it at an expense which I could ill afford.

Once returned, Bill was pleasant enough and invited me up to the house for a cup of cocoa. When I entered, the women immediately noticed my new clothes and examined them admiringly if briefly. Later, as I walked back to my cabin, however, I carried with me an awareness of a slight tenseness in the women's attitude as though somehow I had stirred some fear through such evidence of my expanding loyalties.

I built a fire in the stove and for a long time lay on my bed thinking of Celine until she changed in my imagination to a far more beautiful woman with whom I traveled night after night further into the silent forest.

13

THE little lake had frozen over by the middle of October as I was startled to discover one morning when I saw several Indians walking across it, widely skirting the outlet where the slough had already ruptured a temporary covering. The temperature periodically hovered around zero but rose again in the midday sun to dampen the surface of the snow.

Bill, suffering from what he termed lumbago, had taken to spending the evenings in my cabin, mostly listening to an account of my struggles and adventures through the short span of my life. I soon discovered that he had an astonishing desire for the more formal types of knowledge, which once offered, he judged and sorted, packing the parts away in an orderly brain. Self-educated beyond his secondary school training, he had obviously taken advantage of every opportunity to acquire information, learning French from the priests, and whatever he could of the specialties practiced by the occasional wanderer who had come his way. His cautious check of my data, always approached with rare courtesy, forced me to be careful of my own statements and engendered the greatest respect for his intellectual abilities.

We would sit by the hour, each on a box, our conversation punctuated by periodically stoking the stove, rolling cigarettes, or pouring hot water into tin cups containing a mixture of cocoa and sugar.

He told me of his years as a trader in the big Hudson's Bay Company posts, information which crystallized for me the history of the search for fur as it encroached more and more into the last cul-de-sacs of unknown territory. He described how ten years previously he first made contact with completely primitive Eskimo on the edge of the Barrens who gladly gave a prime white fox skin for the priceless marvel of an empty lard pail.

We became excited over the merits of rare skins which individually brought a fortune in the old St. Petersburg market, where Russian nobles vied with one another to obtain the fox with the longest mane, shining and black.

Bill explained to me that he ran a trap line northwest of the Lake and agreed to take me with him on his first trip over it. The prospect intrigued me as I needed some activity to break the monotony of my life at the Fishery where everyone was depressed by the slowness of the freeze-up and the consequent lack of dog food.

The open water and melting snows made travel difficult, but nonetheless almost half the Indians had left with seven toboggans one day in the hope of finding fish in a district called Among-the-lakes, fifty miles to the north. From there they would move on to their trapping country and then, after two months, meet again at that rendezvous before returning to the Fishery on their semiannual journey to the trading post on the Mackenzie.

Some days when I was lonelier than usual, I called one of the dogs into the cabin. Whitey would sit beside me at the table but after a short while he would begin to pant from the heat and want to cool off. Peter, on the other hand, liked to stay inside and, once comfortable, did not wish to go out at all. I would have been more sympathetic if on warming up he had not taken to letting wind frequently, which smelled up the room even beyond my easy tolerance.

"Peter, you stinker," I told him, "now you have to get the hell out of here so I can breathe." He would put his head down and half-stumble over the sill as I opened the door.

He accompanied me wherever I went for he was perfectly obedient but I had to chain him at night or he would roam, causing all the other dogs in the community to bark. Being a cut dog, he did not fight with them but they became uneasy, if not envious, and if another pulled loose from his chain, there was sure to be trouble.

During the fourth week in October, ice began to hold on

the slough and the big Lake froze for several hundred yards offshore. I had pulled one net ten days before when Pierre, becoming nervous, had lifted all of his, but I had gambled profitably on the other, taking on the last visit sixty-eight whitefish besides two trout, one of which had drowned. We of the Fishery had at least one standard toward perfection in our food—we ate only the fish with bright-colored gills showing that they had been caught within the hour. The others were put away for the dogs.

Cold weather brought some advantage. It was no longer necessary to hang the fish to prevent their spoiling and, at Bill's suggestion, I simply counted mine and threw them up into his cache where they froze into a solid mass. When I had repaid Celine, however, I had less than two hundred which in my ignorance I hoped would last until the nets could be replaced.

The net I had last removed was a dirty twisted mess which I had difficulty in shoving under my bed where it remained unthawed until I could find the means of washing it, another almost impossible task in a house too small to spread it out to dry. Thus harassed as I was with complications, the duties incumbent upon a fisherman appeared interminable.

Bill came in one afternoon to say that he expected to leave the next morning to go over his trap line. This good news lifted my spirits and I spent the remainder of the day in making preparations. Only after an hour in bed did my exhaustion overcome my excitement.

To my surprise it was already light when I was wakened

by my friend's son and told that his father had another attack of lumbago. My sympathy was not aroused perhaps as much as it should have been for I had discovered that Bill had a weakness for which he trusted his generally superior knowledge to make amends. He liked to procrastinate.

I ate a late breakfast and then as I walked around the camp, hoping to wear off the disappointment, it suddenly occurred to me that I could go without him. When I thought it over, the idea became irresistible. I had been living for over a month entirely within the radius of a mile, backed up by the big Lake onto a point of soggy land and barricaded from behind by thickening rows of trees.

We had discussed the trail, over hill and across lakes, the clumps of birch and the brûlée, until I could almost see them. For a quick moment there flashed through my mind the thought of being lost in those dim woods with the snow filling in the tracks behind me but I tossed all fear aside as the sunshine bathed me in a sparkling shower.

I told Bill of my intention. He looked at me, surprised only for an instant, and immediately proceeded to go over the landmarks which I should follow, cautioning me against one place where the ice on a creek might still be thin. In another fifteen minutes, I had harnessed the dogs and was speeding over the wood trail toward the timber.

Instead of following my path up the hill, we turned off, bearing slightly to the west to cross over a low place in the ridge. The dogs slowed down in the unbroken snow, hesitating as if they remembered all at once that pulling a toboggan could be heavy work.

Peter kept turning his head to look at me about every hundred feet, manifestly wondering if I knew where I was going but aware that in the larger sense, the responsibility was mine. The realization struck me very clearly that the dogs would not want to be alone in the woods, especially when tied up to a sleigh, as they were deathly afraid of wolves. I preferred their company also and glanced at my ax and rifle, slipped under the lashing lines binding over the top of the load. I shouted at Peter in confident voice that if he would attend to his own business he would have nothing to worry about. Apparently he was content for once we had passed the height and dipped into a pleasant valley, he led the others at a fast pace over nearly open country.

We had traveled about an hour, zigzagging through a forested section, then across a strip of barrens which I had been expecting, and on into a brûlée. This burned-over land had a unique personality of its own, gray and white where everything was dead. All around straight branchless poles stood like the stubby quills of a goose from which the feather vanes have been singed.

As we went deeper into this monotonous land of silver sticks I wondered whether we were traveling straight. I had taken a compass bearing as we entered and now looked back along the snow ribbon we had pressed, but it twisted incalculably as Peter intuitively sought out the most open course to follow. The trees were not tightly enough spaced for a trail to have had to be cut.

When we stopped, I realized that in a sense we were lost, not really lost but rather alone. The dogs and I knew where we were, each in a comforting relation to the other. It was the world that had become isolated, the villages of people, the towns and the cities, all smothered in snow somewhere behind us. The sensation was curiously captivating.

As I sat on the toboggan a Canada jay flew down and perched on the top of a broken pole to look at the intruders. Here and there on the glistening surface of the earth appeared the tracks of tiny animals which had scurried away at our approach. Seeing them for the first time I began to realize that we were not even truly alone. The midday sun shining above was itself invisible as its course to the south passed below the screening tops of the trees. With a last look at the thread trail we were unraveling behind us, I gave the signal and we moved ahead.

Before long, a slackened speed showed that we were almost imperceptibly climbing. Gradually, a growth of young aspens began to spot the slope and breaking over a ridge we looked down on a flat oval patch of snow about half a mile in length. Clumps of willows along its edge, together with its unbroken flatness, proved it to be a lake.

The dogs enjoyed the open view as much as I, and Peter cunning with years, veered sharply to the right where he had sensed a passage through the brush. I jumped onto the back of the toboggan and we raced whipping through the willows down onto the ice.

There I called a halt and, ordering the dogs to lie down, walked back with my ax to the shore and cut a stubby spruce sapling. This I dragged out to the sled and set it up like a Christmas tree in order to mark the end of my trail which in the windswept open could soon be obliterated.

We crossed the lake and located the little valley through which we were to find our way. In less than an hour we reached a second lake and followed it to its end, making short and visible portages down through a chain of others pleasantly bordered with tall evergreens.

Before the early darkness of the short winter day descended, we arrived at Bluefish Lake, a pond somewhat larger than the others and which had been given a name only because it offered the perquisites of a good camping place a half day's journey from the Fishery. The stand of dry poles behind a growth of fuzzy young spruce could be easily seen along one shore and we pulled in for the night.

The dogs were quite content to lick their paws while I spread my tent over a thick bed of boughs and leisurely put up the tin-can stove, unrolling my sleeping bag on the opposite side. Then I tied the dogs to near-by trees for although I was confident that they would not leave me, I lacked the courage of my convictions.

After lighting the fire I filled my tea pail with snow and put it on the stove, at the same time frying a piece of moosemeat which Celine had given me. The meal proved only a partial success because the tea tasted as though someone had dumped iron salts into it while an acrid smoke almost drove me out of the tent, an irritation I finally discovered to be caused by green brush smouldering underneath the red-hot bottom of my stove.

The weather had turned mild, or so it seemed moving inland from the bitter chill of the open Lake. After feeding the dogs I crawled between my blankets, weary and satisfied. I did not drop off to sleep as I expected but dozed fitfully. Whitey began to bark for some unknown reason. I kept wondering why, and all sorts of strange possibilities pricked at my brain. After what seemed hours, I got up and went to the toboggan where I had left my rifle. I loaded the chamber and brought it in, laying it beside my bed. Then I tucked myself in and slept while the wind howled wildly through the night.

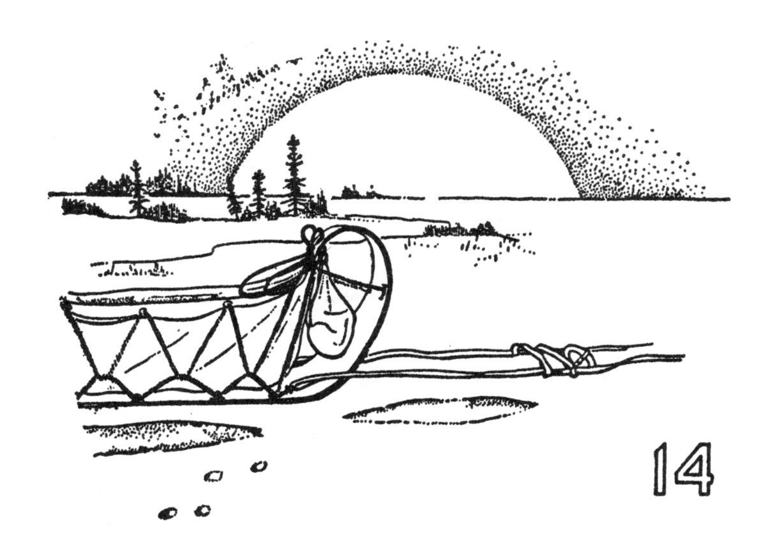

14

TO AWAKE in the complete silence of the winter forest is a rare experience. The air is crisp, the sky is blue, and nothing moves. I shook out my sled wrapper, a nine-foot-long bag of tanned mooseskin sewn in the shape of a sausage casing, open along the top, and with slits at intervals under the rolled edge through which to lace it shut. To balance the load, I put the tent in front of the dog feed and my bedroll behind with the stove and grub bag underneath. Over this equipment, I lay my heavy parka, fastening everything down with the fore part of the headline. When finished, I unloaded the chamber of my gun and slipped it along with my ax under the ropes where they could be watched or quickly extracted if needed. Nothing remained to be packed save the kettles, easily disposed of by dumping them in a sack which was then tied in the cavity under the head of the toboggan.

The dogs shook themselves energetically after a good night's rest, and except Peter, stuck up their tails and bristled their coats in apparent enthusiasm to be off. When I unfastened them, much to my surprise even Peter went immediately to the harness as though looking forward to what the day might bring.

We had turned out into the lake, following it to the end, and had been pursuing our way through open forest for about an hour, when suddenly the dogs began to bark and speed ahead. Shortly I discovered what had excited them for we came to a toboggan trail crossing our own at right angles. Peter insisted on turning into it even after I ordered him across. Finally he went on but before I had realized what he was doing he had circled back. This angered me so I went up and yanked him around, pounding him on the head with a mittened fist. The dogs kept pointing their noses and smelling in the direction he had wanted to go. This puzzled me as the drifted snow showed that no one had passed for several days. My curiosity aroused, I told them to lie down while I walked a short distance to see if I could discover what had raised their interest.

Finding nothing, I turned back but as I did so I saw a deadfall which I had mistaken for wind-blown timber. In it, crushed squarely behind the head was a dark marten worth forty dollars in trade. The animal's tracks as it had approached the bait were clear. It had hesitated a moment, stepped aside, then fallen victim to its fondness for the fish eggs which it never reached. I left the marten and retraced my steps, assuring the dogs that the mystery had been solved. They lost interest, feeling their duty done.

As we went on a few more miles a light snow began to fall. All at once we came abruptly to open country beyond which I could not see. This had been described to me as the Big Muskeg and I had been warned to cut willow wands and stick them in my trail every few hundred yards as I went across. Snow whirled in the wind-swept barrens, bringing me a new sense of desolation. The dogs stood silently, infected with my doubts while I thought of heavy snow filling up the road behind us. There came into my mind a vision of the Fishery and Bill chatting beside the stove. I wanted to go home.

I ordered Peter to circle around which he did, cutting a tight arc and setting off back over our trail at a fast pace. My impression was that he thought I had already gone too far but I reasoned that he must be simply tired of traveling aimlessly around the country.

The snow fell more softly in the timber and we soon reached Bluefish Lake. There, however, our trail disappeared in a light blizzard which was sweeping toward us. The easy portage from lake to lake had changed into a puzzling trap with a multiplicity of trees, some periodically leaning out to hook the sleigh. It required twice as long to get back through the chain of lakes. Peter wanted to turn off but I forced him on.

We had traveled some distance when I realized that we should have reached the last lake but there was no sign of it. When the country inclined upwards I knew that I should have hunted out my old trail and not trusted to my impression that the passage would be so easy. A little further on it became certain that I was lost for the composition of the forest had changed into an almost even mixture of large aspens and small spruce which I had never seen before. I was shackled by the thought the lake must lie ahead.

I began to perspire. Tiny beads of sweat tickled my skin, but my body was cold. I felt miserable. Yelling sharply, I stopped my dogs. Peter sat down, glad to rest. I knelt beside him. "I'm lost Peter, what shall I do?" When I stroked his head, he lay down. Whitey who had been eating snow whined jealously. As soon as I had admitted my predicament and talked to the dogs, the fear passed. How many lakes had we traversed? I could not remember. Obviously we had gone too far without bending to the south.

I reversed the toboggan and rubbing Peter's short ears I told him, "Take us home." He acted as though he didn't quite believe me but he trotted back down our freshly made trail to the last lake. When we were halfway across it, I could see a swerve, the same that he made on our way out. He turned his head once as though to say, "Are you going to get mad this time?" but I yelled "Good old Peter!" and he clipped the corner and headed for the shore.

The view was completely unfamiliar to me and I realized that, excited on my arrival, I had not looked back. I promised that thereafter I would remember always to stop and study the characteristics of a sharp change in our course. As soon as we reached the bank, I could distinguish the gully in the snow that marked our coming. On the ridge, we rested a few minutes while I made tea and scorched some moosemeat in the frying pan. Then we hurried on, the dogs making a purring sound with the even beat of their paws.

Most of the time I jogged a few feet behind the toboggan on my small snowshoes, holding the headline in my hands and letting its end trail out behind me. Intermittently as I tired, I would jump on the empty space left at the rear of my sleigh, just large enough for the front half of my footgear. Since the load was light, my weight failed to impede the speed of the dogs perceptibly. When we climbed, I dropped off, and when we coasted downhill, I rode, for unless I acted intentionally as a brake, being pulled into a fast run became a strain on my snowshoeing capacities.

Although snow fell steadily I was no longer disturbed as I believed that Peter would smell his path over even the windswept sections. At last we wove our way down through a valley and came out on a lake. The wind and snow had wiped out any sign of travelers. Sensuous Peter acted slightly uncertain and I wondered if he could catch our scent through the gusts that whipped about us.

We shunted diagonally across, bordering the farther shore. The temperature could not have been much below freezing for the white flakes were pleasant on the face and the dogs frequently lapped up snow without breaking their stride. Watching them, I did the same, catching a small cone on a mitten and letting it melt into a swallow of water in my mouth. I had learned by so doing never to become thirsty and thus, without being aware of the gratification, to satisfy my need for liquid.

Peter suddenly increased his speed and my eye caught the outlines of our snow-covered Christmas tree, standing up like a welcoming friend to beckon us on. Peter veered sharply and we fairly sailed into the willows but soon slowed down as we started up the elevation, the dogs puffing and panting to get to the top.

After resting five minutes I called to Peter and we set off again in the twilight of midafternoon. The brûlée cast long shadows across our path and I welcomed the open muskeg as easier on my tired nerves. The snow had stopped falling and for a few moments I sat on the load watching an orange sky fade into pink over the distant horizon. My weight made the toboggan undulate over the surface which added a strain to the tired dogs quite unlike my standing on the rear. I soon sprang off, glad to run for the brief relaxation had chilled me.

We eventually glided into the forest again. The dogs kept their pace but I had to stop them periodically for I was suffering from exhaustion. It seemed to me that we had been traveling for hours through this part of our road and doubts entered my mind whether we had not diverged on an uncharted trail. I asked Peter about it but when I mentioned home his ears stood up as though he could hardly wait to get there. Then in an unexpected moment we topped the last ridge and pulled to a stop.

Beyond the lowlands a tremendous yellow moon was rising out of the Lake. I took the snowshoes off my weary feet, stuck them in the front of the load, and sprawled behind on my stomach. "All right, Peter!" I cried and we slid along the slope into our wood trail where, hitting the flat hard surface, the dogs began to race.

Out on the point I could see the outlines of a house showing a small flickering light which grew brighter each second. Underneath me the tough oak boards whistled into the night air as we swung faster and faster toward the camp. I could hear the bark of dogs and then the twinkling gleam of an opening door.

"Whoa, whoa!" I shouted. "Where in the hell do you think you are going?"

15

A FEW days after my return from Bluefish Lake, Bill and I went off together to break out his trap-line trail. With him in the bush I felt no insecurity whatever for he met each situation with almost blasé assurance. The snow had deepened and our movement often became painfully slow, demanding arduous labor in handling the teams. In consequence, our journey took longer than expected and we spent almost a week in covering less than a hundred miles.

The excitement of traveling alone no longer sustained me and I became somewhat morose following his lead. Also I tired of wearing snowshoes and much of the time stumbled along without them. Bill, for his part, was discouraged by finding so few tracks of fur-bearing animals but gradually we set out the supply of steel traps that we had brought with us.

Compensation came in our evening conversations after supper in the tent when Bill elaborated on his knowledge of the woods. I learned simple things such as not to put the tea pail on the fire but to rest it near by until enough snow had melted in it to provide a little water on the bottom to keep the metal from burning which gave an iron taste to the tea. Occasionally wolves howled but Bill shrugged his shoulders.

"As long as you are healthy and with your dogs, you will never get a good look at them although you may hear them cry at night. In my time in the north, I have never been able to authenticate one attack by wolves on a man who could stand up to them, with or without a fire. The only really dangerous animal we have in this country is a mad dog."

Then he told me of an experience that had happened some years past on the Bluefish trail. An Indian coming over it had one of his dogs go mad and turned it loose since the natives strongly taboo the killing of these animals from which, in the mythological past, they believe themselves descended. When Bill heard what had happened he blamed the Indian for leaving the dog where he might have to face it unexpectedly on his trap line, and troubled by the prospect, decided to meet the issue at once. Hitching his team he drove directly to the lake where on arrival he could see the dog's tracks criss-crossing the snow in crazy fashion. He stopped the toboggan and taking his gun, walked down the lake. About halfway he saw the virulent beast some hundred yards ahead. Almost at the same time it sighted him and immediately with a leap it turned to streak down upon him as hard as it could run. Bill dropped on one knee, aiming his gun while seconds passed. At fifteen feet he fired a bullet directly between the eyes.

Going home, still limp from the experience, he met the Indian at the edge of the timber and told him that if he ever let a mad dog loose on his trap line again, he would shoot him first. "Dogs have no fear of man," he added, "and even a scratch from a rabid one may be deadly."

As our days together passed, I became more avid of my surroundings and began to see the forest as composed of individual trees, many of which could be remembered by some disharmonic feature, perhaps a trunk twisted in the middle like a broken leg, or branches long since blown into asymmetric patterns like the green skirts of girls on windy days. These trees I began to know as the signposts of the woodland streets and when we passed them a second time I had a happiness which recognition brings to old familiar scenes. Groves of birch or tamarack, I saw as pleasant parks, hedged by freshly tender spruce, where one could rest in comfort.

Although the return to the Fishery brought relief to weariness, I found myself soon escaping in fantasy to the woods for my superficial association with other human beings tied me down to a painful acceptance of a dull reality.

A spell of unexpected mildness delayed the freeze-up and I went to Pierre to borrow dog food. He was temporarily crippled by a nail in his foot which did not, however, depress his spirits. He gave me all the fish he could spare and later Bill loaned me as many more. Fortunately the Indians killed three moose of which I was able to obtain a share when they traded at the store. The meat proved doubly welcome as it not only provided for my personal needs but gave variety to my tiresome diet.

There was not much which could be done except to haul wood and after I had built up a five-foot pile of logs I became lethargic. One day I sat at my table staring aimlessly out of the window when a little ermine began to play on the snow directly in front of me. In my judgment, it was simply amusing itself for it ran back and forth looking at the cabin like a tourist who has only a short time to visit. I was enjoying this diversion immensely when suddenly Peter charged down upon the ermine and I dashed after him to save my playful friend. When I reached the scene, the ermine had disappeared and I thought the dog had swallowed him. Peter's mouth was clean, however, and with a sudden shift of mood, I chided him for being so poor a hunter.

Another afternoon I saw ptarmigan on the muskeg and I pursued them with the small rifle, but I could not hit one. They did not fly far when they heard the ping of the shot and I kept following, trying to creep close. Except for their heads they were pure white and made an extraordinarily difficult target against the snow in the waning light. Finally I grew cold and had a long walk home, disconcerted by my lack of success.

To solace myself I tried making baking-powder biscuits in the drum oven Bill had found for me. This appliance was constructed of tin in the form of a cylinder about twelve inches in diameter and with a second one inside three quarters of the size. Access to the inner part was gained through a door in the front while the enclosed surrounding area became the divided channel of the smoke pipe two feet above the stove. The biscuits, though heavy, tasted very fine and I was so pleased with myself that I fed one to Peter who had come in during the cooking. He did not like the biscuit which hurt my feelings so obviously that he nibbled away for awhile, finally grinding the residue under the brush on the floor. Biscuits, I decided, were too much trouble and I scratched them off my menu.

Something kept me from any activity for extended periods of the day—perhaps habit holding over from the evenings which were long. Bill had gone out on his trap line again and only from time to time could I arouse myself to build a shelf in the cabin or mend the handle of the bucket with which I drew water from the slough.

One morning I awoke cold and after starting a fire in the stove, crawled back between my blankets. It seemed quieter than usual and when I went outside the dogs' hair was covered with frost. I climbed up on the woodpile to examine the Lake and found it had turned into a pure white sheet as far as I could see. In the stillness I could hear Indians shouting from across the bay. This then was the freeze-up for which all had been waiting so long. The thermometer under the eaves showed twenty-five degrees below zero, but in the new quiet, it did not seem that cold. The sound of the waves had gone and the damp wind also.

The general excitement communicated itself to everyone and I hitched my dogs and started for Pierre's, staying safely on the little lake road. I had just crossed when I met him coming down the trail, happy over the great event.

"Plenty food now," he explained as though making a momentous prophecy. He told me that I could expect at least two hundred fish in a net each day. "Sure," he went on, "sometimes people catch hundreds and hundreds just after freeze-up."

He had worked up the tally to almost a thousand when I threw him into a spasm of laughter by asking quite seriously how many holes there were in a single net.

Pierre decided to return with me but as I wheeled my dogs around, his jumped at them, making quite a scramble until he whipped them off. He was annoyed and blamed me for allowing my dogs to fight but I told him that his had done the attacking and if they were hurt, it was their own fault. Then he accused me of not using a whip to keep my team where it belonged.

This was the first time I had felt the proverbial resentment of a dog driver against one who casts aspersions on his dogs. It was like the bitterness of a father whose children are maligned for characteristics inherent in the young. As I watched Pierre coiling his whip and looking at Ginger, I realized the full force of that magniloquent expression, "Hit me but don't abuse my dog." I had the feeling if he used the lash I could kill him, but the good-humored Frenchman only laughed and I, for my part, felt slightly nauseated from the unnatural intensity of my emotion. I had been too much alone during the past fortnight.

He babied me into demonstrating that I could trace figures on the fresh snow of the lake while sitting on the sleigh. I knew as I outlined a fish that he only intended to make me feel better, but I liked Pierre for his understanding sympathy. Also I had pride when the exhibition was over for no other leader could perform like Peter.

"You should take that dog outside and put him in a circus," said Pierre, clearly impressed beyond his anticipation.

When we had returned to my cabin women could be seen moving out singly over the ice of the bay, each carrying a long ice chisel. "They are setting trout hooks," my companion explained, and again we felt the almost festive quality of the coming of winter.

We had sat down to a cup of tea when Bill knocked on the door. He had just returned from his trap line with four marten and was obviously in the best of spirits. The sudden drop in temperature had conveyed to him a certainty of the freeze-up, an event which greatly relieved his mind for, however little he showed it, he possessed a strong feeling of paternal responsibility for the food supply of the community.

Bill invited us to his house to eat and when we were through brought out a bottle of whiskey, the last of his supply. This unexpected offering completely overwhelmed Pierre who became so excited he almost cried. In the Northwest Territory, each man was allowed a permit for two imperial gallons of spirits for the year, the whole of which was normally consumed in a fortnight spree following the arrival of the first steamer down-river in the summer. For Bill to have saved a bottle might be considered to be one of the most unusual traits of his character.

We talked and drank for most of the afternoon, the conversation finally, as so often, settling on a discussion of trapping and the probable price of fur. Being somewhat out of the swing, both on account of my inexperience and my more limited capacity for whiskey, I went home at suppertime. Pierre stayed on and during the evening I could hear him singing or shouting.

About ten o'clock he stopped at my shack. The liquor had affected him slightly and he told me that he had engaged in a bitter argument with Bill toward whom he felt resentful. He reproached me for leaving and then began to make critical remarks about our host. They were neither overbitter nor entirely untrue but as they made me feel uncomfortable, I protested slightly. This angered him more and he wanted to know why I should make a defense when Bill's wife spent her time in the settlement telling all the Indians of my incompetence, my inability to distinguish green wood from dry, to set a net properly, or even to drive a team of dogs.

I said nothing. I knew that Pierre would go to extremes, and more easily so under the influence of liquor. When I refused to speak at all he went off shouting back at me, "You don' belief me—you crazy in the head!"

16

BILL had arranged for me to pay an Indian woman to wash my nets and afterwards he brought them over to my cabin, she having left them at the store. I had prepared fresh floats and he suggested that one of the men would help me put them in the water for a few plugs of tobacco. As the procedure of setting nets under the ice was new to me, I thanked him for the advice and he offered to ask one of the younger fellows whom he might persuade to take the time.

He did not speak of Pierre and I hinted that our party had developed into quite a celebration. He shrugged the matter off with a shy smile and I concluded that he regarded the affair as unimportant.

Pierre's remarks had made me think about the comments on my lack of skill in all my undertakings. This truth had not disturbed me since such judgments appeared inevitable. The implication that Bill's wife had taken special pleasure in repeating them did trouble me, however, for I was conscious that she had at least a latent resentment of my presence at the Fishery. Whatever her attitude, she had been generous in sending me from time to time a fresh loaf of priceless bread or some other sample of her cooking. It seemed reasonable that she might have wished me elsewhere if only because her husband spent so many evenings in my company. Finding no other easy solution and the subject quite distasteful, I drove it from my mind under the pressure of paying attention to my food supply.

Bill had gone off to talk to some of the people at the store and I began to fasten floats and stones to a net. Presently he returned with a boy named Beja who he said would accompany me as soon as they could find an extra ice chisel. I went on with my work, carefully folding the net on a sheet of canvas. When they came back, Bill stopped only long enough to warn me not to approach the edge of the ice too closely at the head of Great Bear River, where the Lake water, starting on its course to the Mackenzie, never froze.

Beja, apparently content to let me finish my preparations, sat on a box and watched until I handed him some sinkers, whereupon he got down on his knees to tie them on. He lacked the easy skill of my original teacher, and I noted with satisfaction that I had no trouble keeping my side moving as fast as his. Once finished, we folded the canvas over the net and put it on the toboggan together with my ax, the ice chisels, a coil of line, and two heavy willow poles with hooks formed from a section of branch left on the ends. After I had harnessed the dogs Beja sat on the net while I, standing on the tail of the toboggan, gave the signal. We sped down onto the slough, the sleigh whistling sideways as we reached it, forcing Ginger and Scotty to run in a skew curve to keep from falling down. I had practiced this particular start on a few occasions when no one was around and except that I had to drop to my knees at the end of the swing, it was accomplished effectively. When I glanced back, I was disappointed that no one was watching but, once on the straightaway, Beja turned with a look of surprise that I was still with him.

We set our course for the west end of the bay and soon merged with a trail already hardened by those who had gone before. The dogs raced the several miles faster than I could run, only slowing down as we approached the foggy area where we could see several men at work on their nets. The animals were excited, obviously understanding the meaning of our venture and voicing approval by a variety of small noises. At the fishing place there was plenty of room for all and we chose an open section some distance from the others where the dogs promptly stretched out to watch the undertaking.

Putting the net down on the glassy ice, my Indian companion began to cut a hole about two by three feet with the chisel. The new ice chipped easily as he brought the blade down vertically in short, hard strokes, each one splitting off a crystal splinter. In a few minutes an opening was broken through and water came bubbling up under pressure almost to the top.

This part of the labor done, Beja went off to where some other Indians were preparing to leave and soon came back dragging in one hand a long pole, and in the other, what looked like a lacrosse racquet with half its handle missing. With the latter instrument, he began to skim off the floating fragments in the well which he had dug, using care that none of the pieces remained. I wondered at his fastidiousness until I remembered being told that if one cleaned the water of slush with an ice scoop, it would remain unfrozen for a longer time.

When he had satisfied himself, he tied the long coil of line to one end of the pole he had borrowed. This tool actually consisted of three slender rods of spruce lashed together to give it length. When it had been thrust through the aperture into the water, he twisted it in the crotch of one of our forked sticks so that it pointed in the direction desired. Then he worked it backward so that the line tied to the end was drawn under the water. This done, he leaned over and pulled on the line as hard as he could which drove the needlelike rod forward like an arrow, dragging the line after it.

I ran to the far end which I could see under the few inches of covering and began to chop another hole. As soon as it had been completed, Beja reached in with his forked stick and eased the needle along until he could hook and draw up the line. Then he repeated the actions which he had carried out at the first aperture while I went back to feed out the cord, not unwisely remembering to tie the loose end to the toboggan. In this manner we soon had an ice line stretched between the two openings twenty feet farther apart than the length of the net.

At this stage in our enterprise, apparently again some element was missing so we went off in the direction opposite to which we had gone previously. A short distance away we found an old man visiting his net that he had set the night before. I finally made out that we needed a couple of sticks and the old man pointed to the net beyond where we retrieved a discarded willow. This Beja brought back with him and cut it into a pair of two-foot stakes. Driving a diagonal hole at the side of the two net basins, he inserted the sticks so that they leaned over the openings.

Then to finish our task, we tied ten-foot cords from the top and the bottom backings of the net to the straight ends of our crotched willow pieces, then the ice line to one of these hooks. As I pulled at the farthest hole, Beja fed the white meshes into the water through the first until it had all disappeared and I had drawn a hooked pole out at my end to hang on a stake.

Although I was cold from the wind, I stopped to survey the site in reflective enjoyment of an undertaking accomplished. The return trip proved even faster than the journey out and I walked up to the store to see that Beja was satisfied.

"Well how did it go?" asked Bill.

"Nothing to it," I answered, putting my wet mittens beside the stove.

"So there is nothing to it," he chortled merrily, hitching up his pants, "Just you wait until you have to start pulling those fish out of your net."

He gave Beja some tobacco and offered me his can of silk cut from which I rolled a cigarette.

"Whatever you do, be careful you don't cut your line when you chop your holes. After the ice freezes a few feet thick, you will discover that setting a net will not be as simple as it was today. And by the way, don't leave wet mooseskin so close to the stove or it will never be soft again."

As I snatched my mittens I noticed that the tips were just beginning to turn white and rough.

"Thanks for taking care of me, Bill," I hollered back as I went out to quiet my dogs who had begun to threaten a visiting team.

17

BECAUSE of the wind which for two days had been blowing unusually hard, Bill had advised me to wait before visiting my net. He did not hesitate to lend me dog food as the supply commenced to fill the caches, several of the Indians taking nearly three hundred whitefish from a single hole. Everyone in the settlement responded to the luxury of abundance and a dance was planned for the evening in celebration of the winter season.

Soon after I had eaten lunch, Bill came to the cabin to announce that the wind had fallen and suggested that we cross the bay together, there being considerable advantage in having a second person to pull the ice line when resetting the nets. I fastened my mooseskin wrapper onto my toboggan, and hitching my dogs, set out after him on the thirty-minute ride.

I had acquired an ice scoop as well as a chisel and took along a willow to tie to the free end of my ice line for fear the latter would slip through the opening. The ice had thickened and before going on to his own nets, Bill showed me how to cut a little basin extending back another foot from the visiting hole. This would flood, leaving a sink of water in which to pile the emptied net, thus keeping it from freezing into the unmanageable mass which would result from exposure to the air.

I cut my end holes, cleared them with the scoop and, fastening the ice line to the farther hooked willow, dropped the latter free into the water. Then returning to the basin I began pulling pole and line until the net appeared. There were so many fish, I feared my opening was not large enough to lift them through. With bare hands I stripped them out of the meshes, tossing the slippery bodies in a pile upon the ice. The dogs watched quietly with great satisfaction as the fish jumped around, leaving little clots of blood here and there on the fresh snow.

After the first dozen of the catch had been removed my hands became cold in the freezing water and I hugged them under my armpits. The day had seemed very comfortable for at noon the temperature had gone up to zero. I kept on yanking out the fish but occasionally one stuck and I found out that clinging to the prey even for a minute without relaxing my fingers became excruciatingly painful. Periodically I came to a ling which was the worst of all, for the pulpy creature slipped from my grasp and I had to stop several times to dry my hands before I could pry it loose. After a half an hour, my fingers burned as though each time I drew them out into the air I was holding them in a flame. Then when I thrust them back it was like driving icicles under the nails. The torture made my eyes water and I was almost numb from nervous exhaustion when I discovered Bill standing above me.

"Keep your hands down in the water," he warned. "You will freeze them if you don't. It may be hell but the water is warmer than the air."

When a fish stuck, Bill showed me how to ring it with thumb and forefinger over the nose to push the wiggler through the mesh. I had almost finished and his arrival renewed my courage. When the last fish lay quivering on the ice, he pulled the line for me and I fed the net down into the water.

As I dried my hands on my shirttail, he looked at me with an anxious expression. "By God, you're tough! There are damn few white men who can stand visiting a net under the ice in Indian fashion."

My hands felt comfortable and I shrugged my shoulders, still somewhat under the spell of my traumatic experience.

When we reached home I counted the fish while throwing them into the high cache. There were one hundred and ninety-four, two thirds of the number I needed to repay my debts. The situation encouraged me and I planned to put my other net into the water as soon as possible.

As I was about to prepare supper, Bill came over and invited me to his house for the evening meal. Something in his attitude toward me had changed which left a feeling that for the first time I had won acceptance to an inner circle of a strange company of men who live their lives in the north, if not completely alone and independent, then with as little human contact with the civilized world as possible.

For dinner we had ptarmigan which Bill's small son had shot and when our hostess passed me doughnuts especially prepared for our dessert, I noticed that she looked at me for a moment as though I were a man she had not seen before, a person to know if not to like. Before we finished tea, an Indian came in to buy some matches so we took the lantern to the store.

The Indian talked about the dance and I asked Bill if he intended to go but he said that he was tired. We returned to the house and had a fresh cup of tea while my friend described the change which had taken place in the social round of village activities.

"People outside think that the summer in the north is the best time of the year. We do not think so on the Lake. We like the winter nights when there are no mosquitoes or sand flies and the fish are plentiful. Now there is enough to eat for everyone and no one has to work except for splitting a little wood to keep the stove hot."

With that, he moved to the door, opened it, and stepped outside. "Look at that sky," he said, pointing to the heavens over the muskeg. Bands of purple and gold were weaving in and out among the stars like fireweed and goldenrod following a country road.

"Where can you see anything like that?"

He shivered a little and swung his arms, "All free, too," he added laughing.

I did not go back into the house but went to my dogs and hitched to the toboggan all but Scotty whom I told to look after the cabin. I petted him a few minutes, his fur smelling sweetly against my face. He was tired and contented to stay behind. Then we set off down the slough following a good trail across the bay to the settlement. We kept out on the lake until we were opposite Pierre's house and then turned up the sloping shore.

Pierre heard us coming and opened the door to call to his dogs to quiet down.

"Jees Chris'," he said, "you're quite a fisherman. Come in!"

"What makes you think that?" I asked, pleased and yet surprised at the greeting. Celine, too, was smiling as I walked into the room. Pierre went on talking. "They say you take fish out of a net just like a goddam old Indian." Celine, now laughing, interrupted him. "She say they give you a name now—Tsa-djeri, that means 'pointed toque.' "

I realized that my red woolen stocking cap which I had been wearing since the weather turned cold probably stood out in bright contrast to my white parka when I ran over the snow with my hood thrown back.

I asked them if they were going to attend the dance and they replied that they were. I had another cup of tea and Pierre, still joking away, said he was sorry they had no moose nose for me to eat. Celine wrapped a red silk handkerchief around her head, while Pierre put on his parka. "Come on fisherman," he said, "we are going to a dance."

18

PIERRE pushed open the door without knocking and entered the single room crowded with Indians. Of the eleven families living in the community, all must have been in attendance. Apart from the small stove in the center, the little remaining furniture had been crowded against the walls and was now pressed out of sight by the visitors who either sat on it or crouched down in several rows around the room.

A niche was opened along one side and the host made the gesture of ordering some boxes placed for us which we waved aside out of deference to the old men already seated. At first I thought the quietness was due to our arrival but then I remembered that we had heard no noise as we approached. Most of the people said nothing although occasionally someone whispered to his neighbor. The only disturbance was created by the younger children who crawled over each other and vocally protested when stepped on. Here and there a baby cried but was soon hushed by the woman in whose charge it belonged. Clearly the pattern of behavior involved restraint.

I was beginning to wonder what was stopping the celebration when one of the boys at the back of the room got up and began to warm the caribou parchment of his drum over the stove, tapping it from time to time to test its resonance. Two others joined him, each with a similar tambourine-like instrument nearly two feet in diameter and covered on one side with skin.

When satisfied with the tone, they stood up at the back of the cabin and began to beat on their drums with slightly curving wands. At first, nothing happened but after a minute or two a man approached an older woman and they walked out into the room. The invitation was so subdued that I did not perceive how it was made. Others followed choosing partners wholly irrespective of sex. A man named Susi, who was rated highly as a hunter, invited Pierre. They, with half the visitors, stood up in lines of four radiating from the stove.

All at once the drums crashed forth in a frightening din and the dancers moved slowly clockwise in a turning wheel, each dipping a couple of times, first on one foot and then on the other. Their mooseskin soles seemed never to leave the floor. Some followed the tambourines closely which were banging out one beat to the second in completely monotonous iteration. The noise deafened me and there was nothing to do but to sit and watch the endless movement.

After a long while, some of the dancers dropped out, but others increased the scope of their movements, twisting first to one side and then the opposite, swinging their heads and arms in a manner which had the effect of being wild in contrast to the preceding measures. Gradually I became aware that many of the Indians were chanting in time to the drums while couples here and there shouted at each other, their mouths forming words of which I could hear nothing.

Despite my having removed my outer garments, the room had become oppressively hot and filled with the stench of unclean sweating bodies. Smell and sound were battling it out for possession of the evening.

Pierre dropped on his knees beside me.

"How do you like it?" he yelled in my ear.

"Fine," I shouted back.

Only a few performers were left on the floor, by this time carrying out sinuous gyrations suggesting the neurotic.

A ripple of excitement attracted my attention and I turned to see an old gray-haired hunter get up off his box. I had watched him on my arrival rather proudly stroking the few long hairs that grew from his chin. Some of the boys near by began to clap as even the drums calmed down in pitch. The other dancers seated themselves and it was obvious that the ancient one would now perform. Although I could not understand the comments whispered around me, I could see in his expression that he felt the younger dancers lacked the traditional feeling for their art.

As the sound of the drums again increased in volume he stepped out onto the floor holding between his hands a gray silk handkerchief stretched in front of his thighs. Very gently he began the dipping movement on each foot, turning slightly as he went down. For a moment, I felt the pathos one suffers from seeing the physically deficient attempt to imitate a proper form, but as slowly he increased his tempo and began to slide the silken strip from side to side, I realized that here was something new which held the audience in unresisting admiration. Once around the stove and he commenced to revolve in graceful cadence, first in one direction and then the other, like a Siamese temple dancer. Even the children were quiet and I could see the reflecting light of the dim lantern above the stove in a score of fascinated eyes coming out of the human cyclorama which closed in around him like the diaphragm of a camera leaving one brilliant spot of hypnotizing light and sound.

Then he stopped and took his seat, appearing in the minute as though he had never risen. Everyone began to talk loudly, still unaccustomed to the sudden silence of the drums. Some went outside and others moved to join their friends. The old man put his hand on the shoulder of a child that had come up to stare silently at his face.

I looked at Pierre who, always emotional, was tense with feeling. "That old man, he sure can dance," he said.

"Yes, he can dance," I answered.

We went out to relieve ourselves behind the house, feeling refreshed by the stinging air. I asked Pierre how it happened that Susi invited him to be his partner. Then he explained that this evening's performance was a gift dance and that each person who chose another gave a present. I asked what he had received, whereupon he took a plain gold ring from his pocket. This impressed me as a considerable token but Pierre only laughed.

"You see, in this business you got to pay back more than you get and Susi likes to dance with me."

"Well, that is what comes of being a rich man," I commented.

We went into the house again and I looked at one of the drums which a boy was holding. It had been made by bending an inch-and-a-half strip of birch into a circle. Three snare strings crossed the middle of the parchment surface and the open back was quartered with thongs by which the player held the instrument in a nearly vertical position. I tapped it gently with the stick but the sound was flat as the head needed further heating to draw it tight.

I attempted to talk to some of the Indians but my efforts produced only a series of disjointed sentences which accomplished more as social participation than as any realistic exchange of ideas. One of the boys had brought in a fiddle which he had acquired to foster a natural bent for more complex music than his culture afforded. He played a few bars of a recognizable cowboy tune and then offered me the chance to show what I could do, an opportunity which I lacked the ability to take advantage of although it passed unnoticed as the drums started beating once again.

The second dance reproduced the first, the participants perhaps becoming freer in their movements than before. By the time it had ended both Pierre and I had enough of noise for one evening. Most of the men went out again and we went home while the others, drawn by the drums, returned to join the column wheeling endlessly around the stove.

I sat on my sleigh as the dogs made an arc across the bay following the fishermen's trail to its junction with ours from the slough. Overhead the northern lights still pirouetted across the sky like ballet girls with flouncing skirts of pink and yellow. Into my mind stole a beautiful woman dispelling all consciousness or memory until we rose over the bank in front of the cabin. "Wait," I said by the door, "I shall soon be with you."

The methodical beat of the drums continued to roll from out of the night.

19

THE period succeeding the dance was long for night moon following upon moon left only an interim of minutes, meaningless in their monotony, to make up the short December days. The incessant fishing under the ice put a pressure upon the brain: hands burning in the icy water, the numbness for a few hours, the returning ache at night when blood coursed through the fingers bringing anxiety for the morrow's pain. Yet as the hour approached some excitement drew me determined and almost fearless to the nets.

The evenings were my solace and as the Indians became more familiar, my interest in them gained. My brief phrases elaborated into sentences and I began to sense the values which these people, simple only in their material creations, placed upon the crises in their lives. I knew the flutter of rising tension when little Etsele, a slim child of nineteen slipped off to give birth to a baby in the snow unsuspected even in her father's family when she came stumbling home. The old woman who found the baby's frozen body moaned and there was low-spoken sadness in the settlement but no one raised the name of vengeance against the girl who sat silent in the corner, full of grief and puzzled wonderment.

Old Yakudzi made me new snowshoes for the trail, bringing them at suppertime to share my baked fish and tea. "Good snowshoes—à-ne-zo," he said nodding at his handicraft. I puzzled over his words for the low-pitched "à" meant "snowshoes" while high-pitched "á" denoted "fog," just as "jà," on the lower level differentiated "snow" from the upper "já," a a "louse." As though this were not complexity enough, the tone shifted its register when preceded by the pronoun so that "sè á" turned out to mean "my snowshoes," not "my fog."

There was laughter as I learned, but bit by bit I fitted the pieces together until I could catch a meaning in the refrain of a song sung by a girl coming home from her nets through the silver mist of the evening. Etched into my memory became the familiar sound of "se-i-ní-a" with the third syllable hung on the wind to carry across the bay to some chance listener. "Sweetheart" we would say, but in that sensuous tongue, it exposed the richer meaning in the synthesis of its basic elements which simply expressed "that one who is in my mind." Only this burden was given me for the remainder of the melody lost itself in the breeze, leaving me to imagine my own romantic roundelay.

When returning from my nets in the dim light of dusk, I

overtook eleven-year-old Marie, running ahead of her three pups, to ask her if she was not afraid to be out alone, she raised her red-cheeked face and whispered, "My father says that those who fear die young." Then embarrassed, she turned and ran, flinging up her heels to almost touch the woolen scarf that fluttered out behind her. Nonetheless, the next afternoon she came to call with another of her age, both standing quietly some distance from the cabin until I calmed the dogs. They showed me how to make string figures—the pick up on the foot, the saw, the pole turn—although these were properly games for spring. For my part, I fed them hot cocoa and sugar candies until they would take no more and shyly left, marching in single file, heads down, along the trail.

At times I thought the Indians never told the truth. If one returned from hunting and said "No luck," I would later learn that he had killed a moose. The meaning of the common word "sǒ-ni" continually confused me. First I thought it meant "I do not know," later "perhaps," then finally, "I know but will not tell you." In time, I discovered that it might convey any of these three ideas, depending on one's subtlety in interpreting the speaker's emphasis, just as a listener derives a question, an affirmation, or a doubt from the modulation of a "yes." Even more peculiar was the action of a visitor who manifestly arrived on a conscious errand. When asked what for, he or she would answer "e-ku-ri—no reason," and after some delay, explain. Such a case occurred one night after dinner when I had stopped to seek Bill's counsel on a minor matter. An old woman came in and sat down on the bench against the wall. Her obvious agitation provoked curiosity as to what was on her mind and why she came. "No reason," she informed us. After our giving up the quest she suddenly shattered the quiet by demanding help for her child who she said had cut its throat while playing with a knife. We jumped to harness a team of dogs and raced full speed to the settlement. Fortunately, the child's cut was in the mouth and had stopped bleeding of its own accord.

In the middle of the month, Bill went off over his trap line with his son. I, despite my caution, broke an ice line while visiting my second net and could replace it only after bringing the frozen bundle home to dry. Nevertheless, the fish were piling up in the cache by hundreds and all my debts were paid. There was wood to haul and wood to split. I liked to crack off sticks of spruce from the straight-grained section of a log frozen so hard that with a slight twist of the handle when the ax bit in, the piece would fly. Sometimes I helped to swell Bill's heap of kindling which like an Indian's, was always low, but there still remained the long hours of the evening to while away half dreaming in the candlelight.

A week before Christmas when the hour of sun had gone, three teams of dogs arrived from the east. The outlying bands were beginning to collect for the midwinter journey over the mountains to the trading post in the valley. Late the same night, old Kagaye and little Edward drove down the ridge finishing a five days' journey from their camp on Big Fish River. Lights flickered late in the houses and there was a great visiting about. Everyone wanted to know how the trapping had fared in the district and whether the hunting was good.

Each eyed the fur bags of the rest but none showed his catch.

There was much talk in the settlement as to who would be traveling to the Fort. All fall the snows had covered the trail deeper and deeper until no family could have opened a road alone. Eight or more teams taking turns in the lead would break through in four days perhaps. Pierre and Ereya had decided to go from the settlement and there were constant visitors at the store to buy a harness buckle or some extra bit of food in celebration of the journey. The last night Alexi and his family pulled in from Big Bear Point, southeast across the Lake. "Poor catch," he said but his fur bag would have belied his statement if his smile had not.

The annual hegira had held no attraction for me until I realized its festive aspect. Bill was remaining to trade and I had not prepared for the difficult trek in the dark, but as I watched the nine toboggans strung out for a mile across the bay in the late morning dawn, I had a recurrence of that childhood feeling of being left behind.

I spent an hour helping to tidy up the store which had been pulled apart in the last-minute rush to find a box of special shells for an outsize gun. Then we sat and smoked while I refolded each colored handkerchief that Alexi's girl had minutely examined before making a choice to exchange for her bunch of ermine. The quiet which had again come over the Fishery was depressing, and I wandered home after Bill confided that he had caught only one marten on his last week's trip.

Two days later as I washed my cup and single plate from

which I ate my lunch, there was a heavy knock on the door which startled me since Bill tapped softly and the Indians waited for my dogs to announce their presence.

I looked out and saw two mixed bloods who had been trapping to the north. They were darker than Indians and spoke clear English. They were bound for the Fort and asked whether I wanted to join them and said that if I did I could do so when they would pass by again at six in the morning. I saw them off, with carioles bulging, each cracking his whip behind a string of fine big dogs.

When I asked Bill what he thought, he suggested that the trip would be an interesting change.

"The men are first-rate travelers and have two of the fastest teams in the country. They hope to do the eighty miles in only two days and with three sleighs to take the lead, it will be easier. Packing a light load you should hold your own."

Bill helped me turn the mooseskin wrapper into a cariole, bringing me a backboard to slip inside at the rear. It pressed against a cross strut by two stout ropes from the head, each knotted before going through holes at the top and drawn taut through the last loops of the side lines. Once the wrapper edges were lashed over the stretched ropes, I loaded a hundred and fifteen whitefish and put the toboggan next to the woodpile for the dogs to guard.

Bill wished me luck and I crawled into my bunk, filled with excitement to toss sleeplessly for half the night.

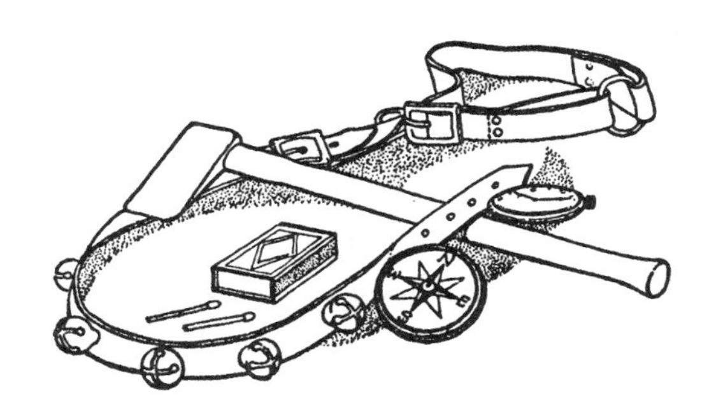

20

DREAMING of clinging to a boat as it plunged through the rapids of Great Bear River, I awoke to find myself being shaken by a stealthy figure in the pitch blackness of my cabin. "Six o'clock" it said, and disappeared. My eyes seemed stuck together but once my eiderdown was thrown from my face, the bitter cold licked over it with icy tongue, washing all sleep away.

Jumping up for a second, I touched a match to the fire already laid and waited for its comforting rays of warmth. Despite the lost sleep, I felt fresh and impatient to finish my packing. Bill had advised me against carrying a single item I would not need and I hoped by leaving my tent and gun behind to limit the load at two hundred pounds. I carefully selected two new pairs of wool socks, putting one on over the other. Then I added duffel slippers and a second set with flaps on top. At least my feet would not be cold if I kept them out of water for I, by the rare fortune of perspiring little, escaped the most persistent danger to winter travelers. I slipped into my woolen breeches, tucked in the shirt in which I slept, and pulled on the mooseskin boots, tying them with long strings around the ankles and below the knees.

Into one sack, I tossed various selections of food in small cans or bags and into another a change of boots and socks together with such essential articles as sewing awl and line with which to mend a harness, an extra box of matches and package of tobacco. I checked my pockets: compass, watch, knife, coil of heavy string, match safe, material for smoking—all were there.

Outside the dogs were stretching.

"How are you feeling, Scotty? Want to take a trip?"

He stretched his front legs forward and his rear ones back, arching his spine like a sagging dryfish stick. Then he gave a vibrant yarr and shook himself all over.

I filled the cariole and went up to the store, where my traveling companions were consummating some last-minute deal in furs. Not to intrude, I dallied around outside in the dark until they finally appeared in high spirits and went with Bill for breakfast. Eating little or nothing in the mornings myself, I joined them for a cup of tea, too tense in anticipation of our departure to think of other things.

It was almost nine o'clock when we slithered down onto

the slough and set out across the bay, my team in the lead to pace the others. For the first half hour we proceeded steadily but I became more and more conscious of dogs pressing from behind. They carried little bells on their harness which tinkled as they ran, the mark and pride of the *métis voyageur*. As I called to my dogs, urging them ahead, I could hear the crack of whips, the shouts and curses which characterized the driving of my companions. Speed and noise for them were the symbols of dissimilarity to the plodding Indians whereas I had taken my precedent from Bill who moved with silent certainty through the forest as though what lay ahead was as unimportant as that behind.

My legs began to ache and my breath shortened from the uninterrupted strain of pushing forward. My heart pounded but I forced myself on and in a few minutes my breathing resumed its easy rhythm under deep draughts of freezing air.

I had followed the trail half-consciously to the south shore and over the flats for a mile when I was called to a halt and asked if I knew where I was going. In truth, I had not given the matter any thought for some time past and by surveying the situation it became apparent that I had drawn off our caravan to follow an Indian's trap line. My fellow travelers were justifiably annoyed, and taking the lead, cut diagonally to the west across the unbroken snow. Fortunately, we had not diverged very far, although I was weary from pulling my snowshoes out of the soft surface before we joined the tightly packed trail which had obviously been the route of many recent toboggans.

We stopped for a few minutes at the edge of the timber, this being the end of the first spell from the Fishery. The rest restored my confidence and for the next half hour, I tailed the others, Peter frequently having to slow down not to overrun the party. Following a team offered an incentive to the dogs very different from setting the pace in front with all the comforting sounds behind them. Gradually, however, we dropped further to the rear and when the sun was at its zenith we reached a narrow lake in fallow country from which the others had already disappeared.

By one o'clock, we closed in on the lunch camp near the bank of Porcupine River which my companions said they had reached some twenty minutes earlier. By suppressing any sympathy which they might have felt for a comrade, they showed contempt for the inadequacies of my performance as it cheated them of the triple rotation in leaders on which they had counted. I did not blame them, and confined my discussion to the characteristics of our route while hurriedly frying a fish in their already heated pan. They were anxious to be off so I gulped down a second cup of tea, and with a biscuit still in my hand, I pulled out on their heels.

We coasted onto the stream, following it down to the left bank of the Great Bear River which still ran open through this part above the rapids. In the subzero weather, I revolted from the sight of deep flowing water as from a horrible and deathly trap. To burn in molten metal would be preferable to the torture of slipping into that rippling steel-blue torrent. Ahead we could hear the dogs cry from the lash as they were beaten unmercifully to keep them from the edge. Peter stretched his head out closer to the ground in fear but when I called to him encouragingly he relaxed, carefully picking his way around windfalls and trotting when he sensed the going safe.

Once away from the Bear, my partners speeded on but I did not urge my dogs, seeking to conserve their strength. It was clear that neither they nor I had been hardened for this race and we had far to go. Also I had been warned by Bill to watch for an overflow from a spring which never froze. With relief I found the place beyond a stand of willows exactly as he said. The road was dry but the dogs slipped on the milky folds of seepage ice.

At Little River, I discovered the remnants of the first night camp of our predecessors, four spells out from the Lake or roughly twenty miles. Bill had explained the measures of native travel when on our trip together.

"About every five miles," he said, "the Indians rest their dogs, making tea where firewood is available. Generally at the end of the fourth spell you will find a suitable place to spend the night. On the trail to the Fort, watch out you do not run past the first one unintentionally for the ten-mile muskeg lies beyond in which there is only a single patch of brush for bedding."

"How do you know the distances?" I had asked.

"You don't," he answered. "Some spells may be only three or four miles apart and others eight to ten but they will average roughly five."

 K

Dusk had drifted into midafternoon starlight as we stepped off again. The forest thinned out into brûlée and we crossed stretch after stretch of barrens. I wondered when we would reach the open plain, for an instant imagining I might have gone astray but there was no mistaking the freshly hardened trail. My left leg ached and began to drag while cold permeated my body, bringing the realization of what it would mean to stop for long without a fire. The fantasy of lying down obsessed me and then I would fling it loose with a shudder. I seemed to have lost all sense of time in the methodical plunging onward.

Then with complete surprise, I saw a fire burning among the trees. As my dogs drew up to it I slipped out of my snowshoes and half-stumbled onto the bed of boughs laid out to windward.

"What happened to the ten-mile muskeg?" I asked, verbalizing the question on my mind for hours.

"You've just crossed it. Where in the goddam hell have you been?"

I did not reply but thought over and over again how much easier it would have seemed if I had only known the route.

We ate and then rested until ten. I learned as I led off that we had been camping on an island in the middle of a lake. At the finish of the next spell, my team was relieved and we started to slip behind. Our way led upgrade through a pass in the Franklin Mountains, pleasantly open country with tamarack mixed with the spruce and aspen. I felt better than I had all day but my knee pained badly and I rested it whenever the terrain afforded an easy transit. I had almost forgotten my partners when I reached them two hours after midnight in the night camp where they had just finished their evening tea. Bothering only to tie my dogs and unroll my eiderdown, I crawled into it and fell fast asleep in the right angle formed by two toboggans.

We arose at dawn and started off without eating, I having left forty whitefish cached in a crooked tree. I felt wholly restored by my seven-hour sleep. The temperature seemed to have risen nearly to zero and I trotted gaily along without my parka, gradually working down from the dark ridge onto a beautiful lake cradled in the mountains. It was a relief to have passed the divide and the bitter cold of evening had become the morning's stimulant. Finishing my spell, I slowed just enough to hear no sound beyond our own. It was then that bad fortune struck me straight behind the ears.

We were sailing along in flat open timber and I sat down backward on the moving load to tie a lacing of my boot. Suddenly the ground dropped from underneath me and I spun head over heels in the air. When I had extracted myself from the pile of snow which softened my fall I saw the toboggan upside down on top of the dogs at the bottom of a twelve-foot precipice. This then was the Steep Bank River to which fate had timed my arrival for the only minute of the journey when I had not watched my course.

I pulled the toboggan right side up while the dogs struggled to their feet and shook themselves, more surprised than hurt. I blushed to look at Peter who gave me a hard stare.

"The headline, the headline," he seemed to be saying, "can't you snub the headline when we go over a dip?" I tried to explain about the shoestring but I could see that it was no use, and proceeded to check on the load. The ax had fallen off but otherwise everything dropped back in place when pushed a little. Then I discovered we had snapped a trace connecting the dogs together.

It took half an hour to mend it by which time my fingers were almost frozen. At least the dogs had rested and I speeded them on. The sun rose and sank again while we twisted and turned through a narrow valley with close-placed trees ticking off our march like seconds on an endless screw of time. It was midafternoon before we reached our fellow travelers hitched and ready to go at the night camp on Loon Lake. They were in a furious temper, sarcastically bickering with each other. The Bear Lake bands had left a tent standing and with the parting advice for me to stay in it, they whipped up their dogs.

I cooked a meal on their dying fire. I was tired and my animals exhausted, especially Scotty who had pulled so hard that he had run half sidewise, taking Ginger's share of the load as the latter weakened. They did not want to go further but I never intended to stay. It was not quite four when I looked at my watch. Run fifty minutes and rest ten, I thought—four spells, twenty miles. We should make it by nine o'clock.

Peter raised himself to his feet one leg at a time and the others jerked themselves up after him. Whitey stood quietly looking ahead while Scotty leaned lightly into his collar, swinging his head with his tongue hanging like the knocker of a bell. Ginger acted the least tired. I patted each one on the head as I walked back to the toboggan and grasped the head-line. "All right!" I shouted.

One after the other the dogs picked up the slack and we moved out into the night leaving a faint glow of coals in the darkening grove. We climbed off the lake into bushy country. The first hour passed and then the second bringing us to a string of little lakes. Scotty weaved in the harness. The air had become bitterly cold and I so dazed from constant running that each footstep felt like a blow pounding on the bottom of my skull. Ginger slackened away from his collar entirely. I took the caribou-skin whip and beat him until he whined and whimpered. We had climbed into the hills when Scotty suddenly dropped in his tracks. I went up and knelt beside him and he raised himself slightly, his eyes glassy from exhaustion.

"What's the matter, Scotty?" I said, taking his head in my bare hands. He pushed it toward me as I pressed my face into the warm fur, stroking him softly. For a moment I felt dizzy and as though nothing else were important. The sensation resembled the embrace of a woman in whose arms one forgets all trouble. I began to dream and then I saw her there smiling among the trees, a figure unlike anything I had ever known. Her dress had an affinity to snow and her face to the tinted wax of a burning candle. I reached out but she shook her head as I fell over on my side.

Startled and afraid, I jumped to my feet immediately knowing that there were no seconds to lose for my body was numb with cold. I slashed all around, the long caribou snake cutting fur where it struck. The dogs leaped forward and we ran for a hundred yards while I felt the blood oozing through my veins. We reached the height and started down at a steady pace. Fear bit at my heels and I closed my eyes trusting the headline as a guide. There she was dancing along beside me with her sweetly wanton smile.

"I know you, snow lady, but I must not stay with you tonight. There's a Christmas party in the village by the River and I am very late."

"Don't be afraid," she whispered.

When I opened my eyes we were on a lake lying on a little shelf overlooking a valley. The bright stars overhead lit up a great ribbon of snow in the distance.

"Look," I shouted at Peter, "the River!"

Perhaps it was the tone of my voice but the dogs' hair bristled and their feet began to patter in speeding cadence. We twisted off the lake and down through a gorge, I riding through a tunnel of willows with head bent low. In half an hour we swept out on a slope where above the trees, we all could see the gold cross on the little Mission spire.

21

AS I pulled up in front of the Mission post office to inquire for mail, I met Pierre coming out, his worried face breaking into a laugh as he rushed up, half hugging me in enthusiasm.

"I just told the Father you'd make it by eight o'clock and if you didn't, by God, I'd go out and find you."

"Thanks, Pierre," I said, putting my arm around his shoulder, happy at the thought that he might have come.

"Those no good bastards, boasting they make a record from the Lake and leaving you all alone on the trail," he went on, his emotions rising.

"They are not so bad, besides I had company enough," pointing to the dogs as an answer to his questioning glance.

"Chris', what a team," he said looking at the four who sat proudly as though they wanted anyone to think that for their part, they could turn around and run the whole way back.

"We go home together," he said, giving me a friendly shake.

"That's a deal, Pierre, providing you won't run off and leave me," I answered, showing pleasure at the invitation.

"I guess we won't be able to keep up to you now." His eyes twinkled and then he broke out laughing. "Wait until I tell everyone you came in less than an hour behind those boys," and he dashed off.

Pierre I suspected would spin a tale but I was happy. I greeted the old Father who was solicitous for my safety and warned me that I should not risk my life traveling alone in the winter nights. I promised to come to midnight mass and with a packet of letters held since early fall, I drove to the barracks.

Corporal Miller opened the door of the trim white painted house as he heard my team turn into the yard, his tall figure silhouetted in the bright glare of a gasoline lamp.

"We are just about to sit down to eat some roast turkey and we've saved a place for you. Constable Crane will put your dogs in the kennel."

I shook hands with both and we went into the small but neatly furnished house. Mrs. Miller came out of the kitchen to greet me. "It's so nice you arrived in time for dinner," she said.

They had festooned the room with bits of red and green paper, adding a baby spruce in an effort to catch the homely Christmas touch. For a moment, I felt strained as we sat down at the table with the clean white cloth still glistening from the iron, the formally placed china. From the corner of my eye I watched the Corporal as he repeated grace, leaning slightly over a bowl of steaming soup, the polished brass buttons shining against the red dress coat of the Royal Canadian Mounted Police. I laid a napkin half-unfolded across my knees and following our hostess' lead, began to eat.

The food was excellent and I soon warmed to the gaiety of the occasion, responding half-coherently to their curiosity about my experiences and the country in which I had lived during the long six months since last we met. As I answered their questions suddenly I had the feeling of trying to describe a world so different that I could neither carry them across the gulf that separated it from theirs, nor in this comfortable home, wish myself returned to that already dimming memory of another land.

Perhaps they noticed lines of pain in my tired eyes for the conversation shifted to the little incidents of the daily round of family life.

"How do you like the turkey?" the Corporal asked.

"The best I ever tasted," I responded honestly, accepting a second heaping plate.

My friends looked from one to the other with an obvious secret thought among them. Slightly self-conscious I said that I hoped that I had not eaten more than my share. The size of the remaining platter proved their protestations to the contrary.

"How did you get the turkey?" I inquired more to further

discussion than out of actual curiosity. There was silence for the second and the Corporal blushed slightly as he smiled.

"That's roast lynx you are eating. I hope you like it now you know."

We all laughed heartily at my innocent acceptance of their spurious bird. Perhaps weariness as well as the cranberry sauce had its part in duping me but we all agreed that the flavor was remarkably akin to turkey although the texture matched the rich white meat of a freshly roasted loin of pork.

After the dishes were washed, the Corporal played on the portable organ that stood against the wall while his wife sang Christmas hymns, the Constable joining in to swell a familiar chorus.

At midnight we went to mass. Everyone in the village had come and even a few teams of dogs were tied to the hitching posts. The posts shone like heavy yellow stalagmites, their bases big with frozen urine. The overcrowded room was hot and smelly and in my drowsy state, I almost succumbed to sleep before the brief service had ended. The Father would understand, I thought, even should my seeming lack of respect embarrass my Protestant friends. Crane took me to the Barracks with him and I fell into a nine-hour dreamless slumber.

The sun was up when I walked out of the small building, white painted like the other, which housed the constable and provided a barred cell for the occasional prisoner. I went to visit the dogs who greeted me enthusiastically, apparently fully recovered from their exertions. I petted each and staid

Whitey delighted me by jumping up of his own volition and resting his forepaws on my chest. It was almost a shock to find him as tall as myself. He dropped off, standing very straight and looking at the others while I slapped his flank. It was clear that he had settled any question as to who would boss the team.

I returned to the front of the houses where I could see the whole village laid out on the slope gradually rising from the thirty-foot bank of the Mackenzie just above its confluence with the Great Bear River. The Police buildings stood at the northern end on the highest level with the Catholic Mission in the center and the white-fenced Hudson's Bay Company post finishing the arc as it curved into the river a hundred yards beyond. These three well-kept headquarters overlooked the thirty-odd cabins below, just as in large measure their occupants dominated the lives of the remaining inhabitants.

Near the middle of the ramshackle dwellings on the lower level was the superior construction of one of the independent trading companies which housed the manager and his wife and further along the home of a Syrian fur buyer. With one more trader, these comprised four of the eleven white residents among a fluctuating population of several scores of Indians.

After a big Christmas dinner, with my hosts I went to visit Mac and his pink-faced Scotch assistant at the Hudson's Bay. The former was in a sour mood as a price war on furs had started in the settlement. Offers had jumped fifty percent and Mac would not pay sixty-five dollars for marten or seventy-five for lynx. He was losing the hunt and he did not like it. I sympathized and after a while moved on down the hill to the Northern Trading Company where the manager and his wife invited me to supper. For them too, life had been a strain and I could understand that for a woman, the restricted round of social activities became a serious deprivation. Their large black and white cat which sat on the stoop aroused my admiration for how it survived in a community of mongrel dogs I could not imagine. The owners claimed that the dogs were afraid of it but I reserved my judgment.

We talked of the previous summer's epidemic when twenty-five Indians died in the single month of July and how half the whites had remained drunk for weeks while winter supplies had floated from the beach in a disregarded rise of water.

"That is life in a trading post," said my host laconically with a smile as though the memory of the annual bacchanalia held some measure of relief from the dreary changeless days that followed. "It wouldn't have been so bad if the boys had drunk the whiskey and let it go at that but then they began on the extracts, which drove them nearly crazy. You may not believe it but a couple of them finally took to swigging that cheap perfume that comes twelve vials on a card in six flavors—rose, hyacinth, lily of the valley, and the like. My God, the smell was beyond belief, you could not even approach them!"

"Things quieted down while everyone recovered," his wife added, "and the fall was real pleasant and friendly but now that this crazy competition has started, half the men are angry and the others are scared of taking sides."

Her husband laughed nervously and took me into his warehouse. There hung beautiful glistening pelts by the hundreds, soft against the touch.

"You've done all right," I said appreciatively.

"Well, I deal mostly with the Mountain Indians from across the Mackenzie. They are a better breed of men, skillful hunters, and honest. I stake a few and they can always be depended on to deliver a good catch, but if this cutthroat buying continues, I don't know what will happen."

As I walked back to the Barracks in the late evening I turned and looked at the distant mountains towering beyond the River. The sky was clear and a small white moon with a cluster of starry helpers was sweeping the phosphorescent snow. "It must be nice in the high hills," I mused. "Here there is too much talk."

22

TWO days after Christmas I left the post for Great Bear Lake. The trader's wife had given me a cake and my hosts three loaves of bread with a pail of oatmeal cookies besides a caribou leg for Bill. The long line of Indian teams had climbed the hill before noon but I had waited, impelled by some innate desire to go my way alone.

The sun spilled over the western peaks leaving a yellow glow as we trotted along the rim of the village. Peter astounded me as he turned the team aside for a moment in a sudden dash at a mangy dog standing forlorn in front of the Mission church but ahead of my yell he curved back into the trail without breaking his gait, the surprised object of his attack screeching as it fled. "That's right, Peter, clear the road," I cried, chuckling at his impudence.

Veering into the willows which closed above like the loose woven tunnel of a fish trap, we moved at a speed that made their free ends whip against my protecting arm. I was glad when we reached the open plateau of the first lake and stopped to look back over the valley, now misty in the moonlight. With one spell behind us and only three to reach the rendezvous I had a sense of leisure as though a twenty-mile run after the dogs was scarcely an effort to deserve deliberation.

Sitting on the sleigh as we crossed the ice, I thought of the girl who had seemed so real on my outbound journey. I searched both shores but there was nothing save trees stretching out their arms in the near shadowless arctic night. I laughed at myself for being a fool and rolled off the load onto my snowshoes catching up to the dogs' pace before half the headline had slipped through my hands.

As I ran, my mind lingered with thoughts of women, first this one that I had known and then another. These were pleasant memories, too often dashed from my consciousness as the toboggan, twisting through the forest, demanded all my attention to keep it sliding freely.

As we drew out onto a larger lake of the chain, I fantasied a mistress lying in the cariole, quietly sharing the luxury of the night. She was beautiful and gay, laughing at the wind which tossed a swirl of snowflakes in her hair. When we swished over the frigid surface she began to sing and I listened, trying to remember where I had heard the song before. One after another, I shifted the form and face but none would remain. It seemed that my mind had lost control of its desire and a more potent force dispersed the dreams. Puzzled by the inconstant imagery, I closed on the toboggan watching while the dark mooseskin wrapper twisted sinuously like a dancer's body. As I stared the woman of the snow suddenly took form, diaphanously resting against the upturned head of the toboggan and impishly whistling the melody I had heard.

I must have yelled for the dogs stopped short. I felt suddenly tired and cold. "Damn this dreaming!" I said aloud, shivering from a momentary chill. Halting the dogs soon restored my sense of reality although I had lost track of what distance I had come. The monotonous rhythm of running along a barely discernible track in the peculiar hypnotizing light had been responsible I decided. I smiled at the recollection, half sorry to have it gone, and called to the dogs to be on their way.

It was six-thirty when I arrived at the camp on Loon Lake crowded with natives and their teams. The tent was full but I found Pierre cooking supper with two Indians beside an open fire. They made a place for my bedroll and I crawled onto the brush after leaving a score of frozen fish to thaw at the edge of the coals. I took a proffered cup of tea while Pierre jokingly helped himself to the pot of boiling meat and passed his plate to me.

The Indians had traded caribou from their mountain relatives and accepted our eating it as the unquestioned right of fellow travelers. They would not have thought of offering food any more than they would understand an unfamiliar white man's charge of stinginess for the lack of doing so.

The burning wood smelled sweetly pungent and the tea, sprinkled with vagrant spruce needles had become flavored with their resinous oil.

"This is the life," exclaimed Pierre happily, using my shoulders to rise. "Three days and I don't care if I see that Fort never again."

The camaraderie of the bush was irresistible and I thought of Pierre passing his just-used plate and fork with the simple sense of sharing and sweet good will one seldom finds over the finest Irish linen.

After a second dish of meat I fed my dogs the fish now limp and sticky, and returned to stretch out next to Pierre, there to sip a last few cups of tea before the fire died.

"Pierre," I asked, "do you ever think of women when you travel?"

He laughed. "What else does a man think of in this country. Fur and fish perhaps!" Then he laughed again.

"I understand what you mean, Pierre," I said slowly with a smile, "but there is something strange about this thinking. Sometimes when I run behind the sleigh I dream of a girl that I have known, but then out of nowhere comes a woman who fastens upon my imagination until I am dizzy with exhaustion. It may sound silly but she is more alive than any memory."

I could hear Pierre breathing and he looked at me nodding.

"It was like that for me too once," he said. "I called her *femme de neige*—the woman of the snow. Then I met Celine." His eyes twinkled. "Perhaps you sleep alone too much, maybe?" We both laughed until the Indians jerked restlessly in their blankets.

"Maybe so, but I'll have to risk myself with this Neidja—or whatever you call her—for awhile," and still full of merriment we crawled into our blankets.

The Indians made fire at three, cooking fish for breakfast. Pierre said that they were going through to the camp in the middle of the muskeg so as to reach the Fishery on the following day. I agreed to carry fifty pounds of flour for one of our bedmates and after they had gone Pierre and I sat around for an hour to give the caravan a long head start. Then we followed, Pierre setting traps along the way.

By the time we had reached Poor Fish Lake, high in the pass, my knee was paining badly once again and all the joy of traveling gone. Pierre showed consideration and we rested long over lunch, finally moving on slowly until the cold, striking together with dusk as we crossed over the pass, forced us to run more steadily.

We did not reach the camp until eight in the evening. I ached all over. The pain was so intense that tears came to my eyes while Pierre fed the dogs.

"I guess I'm no good for this country," I said despondently.

Pierre suffered sympathetically. "Anyone who can follow a toboggan thirty-five miles over a mountain with a bad leg has no need to say that. I'll bet you there isn't another white man in a thousand miles who could have done it." Pierre's exaggeration turned my tears to laughter in which he joined.

I lay down in my eiderdown between an old woman chewing tobacco and a girl just married at the Fort. Too tired to cook, I had placed three biscuits to thaw out against one of the stove supports in the center of the big tent. The Indians were all asleep and I could see the bare feet of several hunters stretched close to the warm metal, still full of glowing ashes, the sign of an early start. In a few hours the red coals would burn out, the tent air would become bitter, and their freezing toes would wake the sleepers. The old woman breathed heavily but still chewed away. I raised myself once to feel if the biscuits had softened but they needed a few minutes more and I counted them off to mark the time. Just as I considered reaching for my supper, the old dame lifted her head and squirted a stream of tobacco juice sizzling against the stove. Then she sank back, gently snoring.

I leaned over for my biscuits, now warm and soft. Turning their crusts toward the stove I could see the brown juice rolling off like too thin frosting. The idea occurred to me of going out to the toboggan for more. Then I gave up the thought as easily as it came, and wiping the biscuits carefully on my trousers, I munched my supper.

The Indians were up at two but Susi gladly left his tent for us to bring along so Pierre and I rolled over for another three hours of sleep, finally breaking camp at six. My body was so stiff I could not run with speed enough to keep me warm and when at dawn we came on the still red remnants of a tea fire,

I was glad to rest again. By the time we departed I felt much better and took some pleasure in recognizing the now familiar landmarks of the trail. Just as the sun turned on its downward course, we came out on the open muskeg bordering the Lake. Some of the Indian teams were beginning to cross the bay and my dogs, anxious to be home began to race against the wind, not stopping for those in front, but breaking trail in gentle arcs around them, until we rushed up from the slough to the little cabin door.

23

AFTER my return to the Lake, I slept for sixteen hours straight and then wakened only for a period long enough to feed the dogs and eat. Bill brought me a pail of water from the slough as I could hardly walk. When I dressed on the afternoon of the second day, feeling quite restored, Bill told me that I had acted dazed the several times that he had come in to speak to me while I lay in bed. I could not remember his visits and dismissed my experience as one would an unpleasant dream.

My supply of cut fuel almost gone, I sawed for an hour, Bill splitting the sections as they fell. He wanted to know more about the price war on fur and I told him what I had learned from the attitudes of those involved. The situation was serious as the competition meant that most of the Indians would be tempted to hold their catch for the highest bidder rather than pay their debt, and in any event demand an inflated value. Then I recounted the details of my journey while he amplified and footnoted each of my descriptions, giving the Indian place names which so often cunningly suggested the peculiarities of the locale. In the end I realized how much my ignorance, pain, and the winter days had hidden from me.

After supper at his house we returned to my cabin with a small bottle of alcohol to celebrate the old year's end. We reminisced of the past months and discussed the possibilities of a trip to Coronation Gulf in the spring. Then at midnight we went outside and fired our rifles in the air. From across the bay the answers came, the Indians, ever profligate with ammunition, banging away from house to house for a full ten minutes until the cold drove them inside again.

On New Year's morning Bill's young son awakened me and I had made the fire when his mother and Cecille appeared to wish me the season's greetings, each bearing to my surprise a gift. There were a pair of mooseskin moccasins, the white top and fringe around the heels embroidered with silk flowers in fifteen colors, a similar pair of slippers trimmed with ermine, and finally a snapshot of my friend Bill ensconced in a decorated mooseskin frame. The women's faces were lovely in happy embarrassment as I praised their skill to hide my true appreciation. The boy's mother shyly turned her head, as she asked me to come for New Year's dinner and then laughing like a girl, went home. I had never seen her face so beautiful and I noticed beneath her heavy shawl that she was big with pregnancy.

The meal provided all the country could afford for the gayest celebration of the year and it was after midnight when I came home in a howling wind to sleep coldly through the night.

The wind continued, forcing a dash for the fish nets in the first lull that followed. Pounding in my haste I broke an ice chisel and went to Pierre to borrow his. Then, as luck would have it, as I smashed through to water in cutting my final hole, the handle slipped from my heavy mittens and went plunging to the bottom of the lake. In that second when I saw it go, my heart sank after it for to lose a chisel was more than just the matter of my shame. Chisel heads were rare that season and it would be a day's work to haft the steel besides my lost labor and chance to clear the nets. With heavy feet I ran to Pierre's, dumping out the story before he closed the door. He shrugged his shoulders but Celine laughed, pulling her apron over her face to muffle her unexpected merriment. I could have kissed her then for thus disposing of my trouble. Pierre easily infected by the mood pronounced it fortunate I had not fallen through myself, then told Celine she would have to fatten me so I would stick out like a cork in case I slipped after the next chisel I borrowed, and thus with nonsense had me stay to dinner.

Such happy hours were short and rare compared to the long days of sitting wind-bound in the cabin when every thought turned black and all hopes froze. Pessimism spread over the settlement when four Indians arrived after forced traveling two days from the north with news that their band was catching only sufficient fish for the men to eat and that the dogs were starving. Such conditions depressed me for hunger still remained in my mind as the symbol of civilized despair or utter degradation. The Indians did not like to starve but shrugged their shoulders. "Kulu, perhaps tomorrow we will eat," they said as though such deprivation testified to the inevitable nature of things.

Some days I read for I had borrowed several books at the Fort to add to my two volumes of poetry. Bill also loaned me the few copies he possessed, most of his small library having remained at the east end of the Lake where he had traded with the Eskimo for several years. Bill had been an omnivorous reader, preferring works on history, travel, or scientific accounts of the country and I regretted that his collection was not at hand. Still, I found myself unable to linger long over the printed page. Deep in me there was too much anxiety to lose myself in books and I was constantly interrupted by the necessity of feeding the fire which varied the temperature from hot to cold as I turned the leaves. Also the light from the candle held in a coil of wire on the wall above my bed flickered and sputtered in the draughts, leaving my eyes weary after an hour of attempted concentration.

Ordinary novels palled for the emotions of the fictitious characters seemed paper thin. I had but to open my door to find enough pain and worry to make their difficulties as irrelevant as the buzzing of mosquitoes on a summer night.

Only Darwin's *Voyage of the Beagle* won my constancy for its release of my ingrowing concern with myself.

When overcome by physical inertia I would face the bitter cold if no more than to play with the dogs for an hour. Turning Ginger loose, I would tease him into springing at me, hitting him in mid-air a glancing blow across the head with my heavily padded arm. We would keep up this game for half an hour, he being knocked into a somersault to land flat on his back in the snow for a bare second until he rolled over and sprang again, growling in mock savagery. Sometimes, in a lust of brute force I let two dogs romp with each other, kicking them in the face when one sunk his teeth into the other's throat, even though their necks were now so thickly coated with winter hair as to almost throttle the aggressor. Bill put an end to my rough-and-tumble circus before we hurt each other, recalling his warning that my playful friends might kill me before they knew the game was over. Thereafter I only fought with Ginger pushing my blanketed fist hard into his mouth when he tried to bite me or dragging him over the snow by his tail when I could catch him unawares. He must have liked it for he never wanted to stop, nuzzling my hand when I ordered him to quiet down.

By the middle of January, the temperature which had been dipping each few days dropped below minus forty, holding the settlement in its stiff grasp. All wind ceased and one's breath purred from the freezing of exhaled moisture. There was no other constant sound save the crackling of smooth surfaces on the saltlike snow. The moon came up over half the southern sky, first yellow, then shrinking into an enormous pearl. Smoke from the houses rose straight like pale-blue streamers, gradually evaporating into the translucent heavens. One's fingers numbed in seconds and burned at the touch of a dog chain. The people huddled in their houses, only going out to relieve themselves.

When the weather moderated, we had a visitor bringing letters from the Fort, a quiet lanky man with an awkward stumbling walk from years on the trail. He combined the best that two races could produce from people of the forests and hardy pioneers. Hib I had heard was first among northern hunters and as sure with a broadax as when looking down the bead of his rifle.

Relaying letters from the annual mail team down the River had not been gratuitous for it was the common whisper that he loved Cecille, although she sat in the darkness of the corner that evening when he arrived. With years of knowing he had brought a bottle of gin hidden for many months to bind his hearty welcome. Pierre came running and the women searched out the ducks which had hung in the cache through the fall to provide a dinner that surpassed all others. Bill, who had just returned from a trip over his line, forgot that he had caught but one marten besides the usual lot of ermine. That was a wonderful evening with the laughter of children at the sly fun we poked at the man who was courting his girl.

Sometimes Hib came to see me when the day's work of hauling wood or visiting fish nets was over. He told me of the habits of moose as one who had learned them well, how unlike the caribou they travel with the wind and not against it, frequently turning their heads to listen as though paying little attention to what lay ahead. Generally the moose move in groups of two or three but Hib once saw a band of six. He claimed it was futile for a hunter to pursue them in the winter unless a breeze was blowing which would smother all noise as these animals can hear the breaking of a match. With too much wind, however, they are hard to find. Then they hide under cliffs where the air swirls the sounds from all directions, or sometimes seek the center of an open stretch to make attack more visible. Except for man, moose fear only wolves and Hib doubted if one wolf could kill a grown animal although he had recently found a place where six had left nothing but scattered mooseskin on the snow.

After a few evenings my mind wandered, weary of listening to the same voice and Hib came no more, but I still remembered the light in Cecille's eyes when she met him walking in behind a load of wood.

Sometimes I drove across the bay to watch the Indian men engaged in endless games of bastard rummy, wagering their traps, clothes, and food. An hour was enough and I would leave, glad to escape from the heat and smell.

Even Pierre was dull and occupied his time with complaints that the Indians lacked ambition and would not work. He lay in bed most of the while and I felt he was talking about himself. His exaggerations lost their humor and when I challenged his statement that he had seen wild muskox south of Great Slave Lake he became bitter and although we parted with the usual tokens of mutual regard, I had no desire to visit him again.

My feelings coarsened as I kept more and more to myself for there was no place to go. I did not wash my face or clean my dishes. Some nights the thermometer read minus fifty degrees, a point below which it did not register. When the temperature rose, the wind howled and it was more uncomfortable for the fine snow blew through the cracks of my cabin until in the morning it lay an inch thick on the floor. One day in such a storm I had to stay in my eiderdown for my stove would not keep the room warm enough for me to sit comfortably at the table. I would say to myself, "For God's sake, do something!" Then I would go outside and see the dogs lying motionless, curled into white balls of frosted snow, unwilling even to lift their heads to look at me. In every house the doors were closed and the windows glazed with ice. Perhaps I would walk toward the timber until my hands grew numb from the necessity of rubbing my stiffening face. Helpless, I would return, cursing the futility of my action. Then hour after hour I would stay in the little room from which I could not see, alternately dreaming and hating myself.

Finally, the storm ceased and the sun broke through the clouds. Hib and the children came over to spend an hour or two in my cabin and then went home.

I hauled a load of wood for I had but one log left. All afternoon I sawed and split the sections until I cracked the handle of my ax on a knotty piece of poplar.

Later in the evening the gang returned bringing Cecille and

Pierre as well. Pierre showed a slight reserve as though our last conversation still rankled in his mind, but he soon was joking freely.

"I hear you're so tough now you don't cut your fish," he gibed.

It was true that I had fallen into the habit of baking fish in the drum oven without cleaning them but I was puzzled by the speed with which such a trivial detail circulated around the settlement.

"They taste best that way," said Hib, innocent of any overtones in Pierre's comment. "The guts give them a rich salty flavor."

He was right as I had learned for myself. After the fish was cooked and split open, the viscera could be easily pushed aside, leaving a faint brown stain with the tang of soy sauce on the adjacent flesh.

Pierre hastened to insist that he preferred cooking our small whitefish uncleaned himself. Truth was always less important to Pierre than participation.

After midnight the girls went home but Pierre talked until three and Hib stayed for the night. In the morning, Bill's young son came over while a girl was born at the Fishery.

The next day Hib started for the Fort but returned after one night to find someone to break trail ahead of the dogs as far as the pass. He asked for the loan of Ginger and Whitey but while he was cutting the chain loose from a stake which had turned into a block of frozen urine, Whitey put his nose down and received a fearful gash so that he had to be left behind. I suffered with Whitey who whined and incessantly licked at the bloody cut.

It was the end of the month before Hib got away with Bill and Pierre to help open the road, the latter wanting to visit his traps. The sun stayed noticeably longer in the sky and I felt that my days of darkness and depression were over.

24

THE mild spell of the first half of February was a godsend. All day long one could see people passing to and from the nets and I piled up fish although I had again fallen into debt for dogfeed. One morning I started out early, lying in the cariole and watching the first rays of the sun making rainbows in the sky. Near the nets there was a heavy mist so that it was possible only to see a few feet above the surface of the ice. Suddenly the dogs stopped, as I thought, for one to relieve himself. When they did not start again, I lifted my head and called sharply to Peter but he did not move. Furious at this unusual insubordination I jumped out of the sleigh and ran up to him where he stood perfectly still without lifting a foot. The strangeness of his behavior killed my anger and instead of hitting him I tried to pull him forward by the harness. He refused to take a step as I dragged him, whimpering slightly as though in terror. Completely perplexed, I wondered if he had suffered some internal malady which paralyzed his legs. Looking about for a solution to my quandary, something caught my eye in front of us. I peered through the fog for a minute and all at once a frightful realization burst upon me. There was no mistaking it. Not thirty feet away I could see the mist coiling up from open water. The thought of that danger was like a nightmare. It had never entered my mind since Beja had cut the first holes for the nets which all during the winter we had never passed. Now I remembered the warning that if anyone slipped over the rim of the outlet where the Lake water rushed down to disappear under the ice of Great Bear River, they would have no chance of survival. I could see Bill's eyes and hear the sound of his voice as he had told me. Slowly I crawled back.to the toboggan and shifted my weight onto it.

"Come gee," I called to Peter and the dog turned in a close loop, pivoting the toboggan at its center. That night I fed him all the fish he could eat.

Bill winced as I told him the story but then smiled, reaching for a cigarette paper. "You're lucky," he said, "the experience is like an inoculation. It will never happen to you again."

We had decided to make a trip to the Fort together during the latter half of the month and I looked forward to the venture. Journeying by dog team had become an end in itself and mobility the preeminent manifestation of freedom. Even in my sleep I traveled with dogs. As with us all, pain proved hard to remember.

Looking over Bill's handful of books, I found the Douay Version of the Bible and took it home to read. It struck me as less turgid than the verses that I had studied as a child, half fearful of their hidden meaning. In it I discovered a source book portraying in deep-color splendor the ancient customs of the Jews, a people heavy with feeling and closely bound by familial duties. The Old Testament Apocrypha enchanted me and I lived with the dark-haired beauty while she plotted the seduction of Nebuchadrezzar's general, but after awhile I tired of this woman, so alien to my land of snows. For me there was still Neidja, the guardian fairy of the forest whose good will I dared not wholly risk by wandering in foreign worlds.

One day I happened to see a red fox run across the muskeg and skirt the shore, perhaps in search of mice or ptarmigan that might have burrowed into the snow to flee the cold. I took my rifle and coming in behind it thought to drive the creature out on the ice. My action was more of a game than an operation to acquire the skin for I was not one of those fabled marksmen who can drop a fox with a bullet through the lower jaw. I missed my chance to shoot when the animal popped above the bank. In a trice it disappeared and then I saw it run as fast as it could for about a hundred yards. There it stopped and looked at me for a minute while I slipped a cartridge into the chamber, foolishly grasping the barrel with my unprotected hand. The fox ran off, hesitating again at twice the distance for a final backward glance, then hastened on to disappear from view.

My palm was creased from the freezing metal and out of curiosity I tapped the gun with my finger tips. The cold steel surface felt like sticky tape and I realized that at fifty below it might well have held the epidermis when I pulled my hand away. Pups I had seen lick an ax that had been used to chop up meat, then run off squealing and sucking their tongues.

When I returned home I found Pierre and Celine waiting for me with a big slab of trout. After we had built up a roaring fire, Celine opened a bundle hidden in a black silk handkerchief and put a pie and a loaf of bread on the table. When I asked the reason for all the presents, they said that they were celebrating their baby's second birthday. Somehow I felt that this was also a gesture of simple friendship, for Pierre and I had survived the darkest months of winter without a serious disagreement, a rare thing for isolated men in the north.

I made a meal from the fresh food and we spent a happy evening planning trips that we would take in the spring, Celine promising to teach me to hunt moose on the hard crust of the late March snow, the one time when animals cannot escape, wearing themselves down as they break through the surface over which the pursuer can run with speed. As I watched them whisk homeward with their dogs, I had a sense of peace with confidence that my future days would prove more pleasant.

On the fifteenth of February, Bill decided that we could leave for the Fort the next morning. I loaded my toboggan with a plentiful supply of fish including some for the priest who had asked me to stay with him when I came again to the River. I bathed as well as I could with a bucket and changed my underwear for the first time in months. Cecille washed and shrunk my red toque and sewed me an extra pair of duffels, which with a dozen socks I bought at the store, took care of my need for clothes. Then I checked my harness and reinforced the tugs. As I finished, I noticed that the temperature had been falling rapidly in a strong northwest wind.

We set off soon after sunrise, Bill taking the lead. After we reached the timber I went ahead, breaking open the trail which had been blown almost completely full. At the end of the second spell we had tea. I had left without breakfast, and now found that I was unusually hungry, which Bill attributed to the cold. Even the fire which roared on an eight-foot front could not keep us comfortable for if our faces roasted from the heat, our backsides froze.

When we turned from the mouth of the Porcupine onto Great Bear River we found it frozen solid and ran along it easily to the place where the trail turns inland. There, with a load of several hundred pounds of fish, my dogs hung themselves on the top of the steep bank for those behind were climbing almost vertically and those in front were pulling away from the line of least resistance. I hauled from above with the headline and once we surmounted the ridge, the heavy sleigh leaped forward crushing the tip of one snowshoe as it bore down upon me.

Little River had flooded during the preceding period of mild weather, and chopping a hole we found a safe three inches of ice covering more than two feet of water below. Thirsty, I took a drink which left an extremely bitter taste in the mouth. Weary, we pitched our tent after nine hours of traveling over the first four spells.

We had a hard day across the ten-mile muskeg, Scotty sometimes lying down. It was seven-thirty in the evening when I finally caught up with Bill who already had the fire going at the halfway camp at the pass on Dark Ridge. We each made a second cache of twenty fish, tying them in burlap bags to the ends of long poles which could be leaned high in the crotch of a tree.

Bill was tired but kindly and the crow's-feet fanning out from the corners of his eyes looked deeper. All day it had been nip and tuck to thaw the face, each of us constantly grimacing to feel the stiffening cheeks, then rubbing hard, scarcely with time enough to warm the hands in woolen padded mittens before repeating the act again. I wondered how many thousand times it took to line a face like that.

"You have had an experience today, my boy, whether you know it or not," said Bill. "I have never traveled in colder weather. A man could freeze on a night like this without ever feeling a thing."

The air hung so bitterly around the tent one could almost sense its pinch. Before we stopped, I had noticed my breath rattle like sliding ice on a roof and when I had struck a match I found I could not hold another until I warmed my fingers.

We set off early in the morning, my dogs soon lagging behind again, but after a third night on the shore of Loon Lake we reached the Fort in the middle of the afternoon. The valley was slightly warmer and I had put a snowshoe into an overflow at the mouth of one of the smaller lakes but the water had not reached my foot. Bill stayed at the Hudson's Bay and I went on to the Mission.

"I am glad to know you are traveling with a good man," the Father said with sincere concern as he came to greet me. "It was fifty-two degrees below zero here last night."

We stayed a week while the weather moderated although as is usual after one experiences an extreme, we thought no more about it. On the journey home, Bill watched my dogs and then one night in camp told me hesitatingly, like one who mentions an unfavorable incident to the father of a child, that Ginger was plainly loafing. With Peter under-strong in a team of four, it made a difference if the heaviest saved his strength.

"What shall I do?" I asked him.

"It may seem cruel," he answered, "but I would take a dog chain to him. Just be careful you hit him over the shoulders because if you strike him above the kidneys, he may be ruined. They don't feel a whip except on the ears or nose and you'll wear yourself out if you follow the Indian custom of lashing a dog all day long. One good beating and you will find the rattle of the links sufficient warning." He smiled slightly as though he had imparted a dangerous weapon which he hesitated to entrust in the hands of another.

"I'll try it," I said, though I doubted somehow that I would.

All the next day I watched Ginger slacken ever so slightly in his collar, cunningly hiding the negligence by keeping his neck strap tight. For an hour I whipped him intermittently whereupon he would arch his back and throw himself forward for a few minutes while Scotty would straighten out in the harness. Then in a little while he would forget and look for birds in the trees as we passed.

It was Scotty's going down, working himself to death, that got me. I stopped the team and pulled a dog chain out of the front of the wrapper, doubling the ends around my mitten and walked up to the dogs. Peter turned his head curiously and half afraid. Scotty and Whitey relaxed on their bellies, the former chewing snow while the latter cleaned his paws. Ginger just stood there looking at me to see what game I had in mind.

The first blow caught him in complete surprise. At the second, he leaped, almost catching my wrist which startled me. Then he thrashed around until I beat him down into the snow.

When I went back to my sleigh I tried not to think about what I had done and called to Peter. We sped along, Ginger digging into his collar so that the other dogs had to break their pace to keep ahead. Occasionally Ginger gave a slight jump as though to shake himself but except for his will to work, he showed no other sign of his recent experience.

I was surprised for a moment when we caught up to Bill. I told him what had happened.

"I don't think you will have any more trouble," he said. "Tomorrow, hitch Scotty in behind Peter where he cannot take so much of the load and I believe your problem has been solved."

We made the return easily, sleeping only twice, and I felt deeply grateful to my friend for that fortnight we had spent together. My reaction was like that of one who is graduated after a long and arduous course of study knowing that he has learned his lessons well. I sensed my growing competence as a winter traveler but my pride was centered in the realization that fate had given me as teacher, the master of them all.

25

THE next morning I drove to Pierre's as I heard that a prospector had arrived from the Dease Bay country. I found the two men lying on the bed with faces flushed. Celine looked worn and the cabin had an untidy appearance that I had never seen in her house before.

The visitor I knew by reputation. He had not come in contact with a settlement for over a year and a half and until he had made his two-hundred-mile trek from the end of Great Bear Lake he had seen no one. I was glad to meet such a man and gradually I pieced together the story of his coming. He had arrived two days after our departure and gone straight to the Fishery, Bill having staked his ventures in the east.

Bill's wife had fed him and then offered him my cabin to

use until we returned. After one night alone he had sought out Pierre who, immediately responding to his need for human sympathy after so long an isolation, took him in. No difficulty would have arisen if the prospector had not been anticipating his annual case of whiskey which Bill had promised to hold for him.

When Pierre discovered that in all probability the liquor had reached the Lake, he suggested that they go and get it, which in ordinary circumstances could be considered a reasonable proposal.

Bill's wife, it seemed, either because she did not know where the liquor had been cached, or perhaps since she was not aware of the transaction told them to wait until her husband returned.

Thus foiled they spent another night becoming thirstier and thirstier, the one pressing his rights to the other and Pierre, no doubt raising the issue to a point where the delay begged to become the outstanding injustice of Christendom since the sack of Constantinople by the Turks. In any event they called again, this time presenting the case as an illegal withholding of private property. Challenged in this way by men, the woman gave in and they hauled a case of liquor out from underneath the bed and took it home.

Ten days later there was little left but empty bottles and two men hoarse and ragged in their speech from want of alcohol.

In part I sympathized and might have seen the situation in its humorous aspect had it not been that the long-drawn-out reaction from the drink had turned to bitter resentment of the woman from whom they gained it. Pierre started in to tell me what he thought of Bill's wife, his emotions rising with every statement.

"What sort of woman you call that who turns out her husband's partner when he hasn't seen no one for a year?" he asked.

I shrugged my shoulders.

"She's too goddam stuckup anyway, blowing off her mouth about everyone in this place."

Watching Celine's worried face, I could see that he had struck a sympathetic cord for there was a deep ingrained conflict between these women who had married white men. For Celine, Pierre was a child she had taken in, and warmed, protecting him with her superior knowledge of the strange environment to which he had fled. She was proud of this fugitive that her Indian skill had won and loved him with a passion he had taught her. The other woman had been raised in a River mission in an atmosphere of foreign arrogance. Adopting what she could understand of alien values, she had risen high above the status of her people and stood with conscious pride as the wife of the country's most respected citizen.

"I got dogs more valuable than her, she's nothing but a bitch."

"Take it easy, Pierre," I warned, suddenly resenting the attack. "Do you expect a bunch of women and kids all alone in the house to take in a man they scarcely know?" Suddenly she had become identified with my closest friend, to whom in a sense I owed my life.

"She's not so particular," Pierre went on, oblivious to my rising temper. "All the time when you're away, there are Indian fellows hanging around her house. She's just a whore like all the rest."

"That's a dirty lie!" I shouted.

The sharp impact of my voice shocked the listeners and I could see the others shift slightly as though anticipating trouble.

"You don't need to get tough about it," said Pierre after a minute, swinging his head uncomfortably. "Nobody asked you."

"Okay, I'll leave," and I walked to the door. Pierre followed me and as I turned, he said with a wry grin, "No hard feelings?"

"No hard feelings," I answered but went out.

I had not gone a hundred steps before I knew I had been a fool. Despite his gesture, I realized that I had deeply angered Pierre, and that he would not understand my action. After all was said, it had been Celine who made the clothes I wore and took my side when others laughed. More to the point, I recognized that in Pierre's way of speaking, his slander meant no more than that he did not like the woman for her genteel ways.

After a night's sleep I shrugged the matter off and, knowing that it was Bill's birthday, I took him the presents that I had saved for the occasion. He showed concern over the turn of events during our absence which neither of us mentioned. In the evening Pierre and the prospector arrived and I joined them later in the hope that our differences might be forgotten. Pierre's remarks to me held an undertone of sarcasm and I retaliated by asking how his traps were proving up, having seen Celine leave in the morning for a trip over their line. Also I went out of my way to be friendly to Bill's wife, joking about the incidents of village life, while the others as usual speculated on the price of fur.

When Bill and I were left alone, he surprised me by remonstrating at my behavior, stating that such familiarity could cause gossip in the settlement. I was shocked by his sudden show of temper and, helpless to explain without revealing the complications that I wished to hide, I walked home in sunken spirits.

When I wakened Bill was lighting a fire in my cabin, obviously having come to make the apology he offered for his vexation of the night before. I told him I was sorry and, with the belief that is father to the wish, expunged the incident from my mind. His wife put a backing through a net and I drove off to set it. The devil must have driven with me because I broke Bill's ice chisel and had to return for another. At seven-thirty I gave up for the day having dug a hole four feet deep without going through to water. That night as I came in, the temperature was forty-seven degrees below zero.

The day before he left, the prospector came to see me, bringing as a gift some Eskimo spear points made of caribou horn.

As a result of our disrupted meeting, the conversation proved a strain. Unthinkingly I handed my guest an empty can in which to spit as he seemed to hesitate in spitting tobacco juice on the stove and floor but when he had gone I had the feeling I had erred again.

When Bill did not come to see me I sought him out. He brusquely told me that he was tired of apologizing for my rudeness to everyone. I did not refute my reputation for bad manners but challenged him to say when I had been impolite to him. When he told me that several months before I had spoken of his children as insects, I realized my case was hopeless. I vaguely recalled using the word to describe the appearance of babies crawling on the snow. No offense had been intended and despite the reaction to my simile, he knew then that none was in my thoughts.

I went back to my cabin and lay down in my bunk, realizing that I did not have a friend with whom to talk. There was something strange that I could not understand about the situation, and filled with bitterness I turned to the wall unable to tolerate my thoughts. Gradually as I relaxed, I seemed to hear someone whistling. In the darkness I saw at the edge of the forest a girl in a spruce-green dress standing beside a team of pure white dogs. She waved to me and I ran after her while the fire quieted in the stove and finally went out.

26

THE weeks of March were the worst I ever spent. Deprived of even the intermittent friendly conversations which made our winter struggles a common cause, I felt my ostracism more than if I had been alone. The temperature moderated slightly but the wind increased, roaring from the northwest for days on end and then rushing back from the southeast with a cold feathery intense snow as though to fill the emptiness it had left behind. I came to hate that wind as something wicked. Water thrown out the door fell like hail and snapped vindictively afterwards. For me the minutes crawled into hours and the hours stretched out so long that each was stale and dull when half consumed. There were nights I lay and thought of Neidja beckoning from the woods.

She would come and put her cool hand on my fevered face but would not stay, leaving me with a confused mixture of passion and memories.

When the storms ceased I went to the timber and cut logs, hauling load after load until it blocked my door from view. I got old Towaji to help me set another net, a long and arduous task for now it was impossible to see the needle under a full five feet of ice and consequently useless to jerk it forward with the line. We put down a slanting aperture and paced its length, digging holes for hours. He piled the fresh snow high around the basin opening so I could sit protected from the wind, the dogs watching hungrily the little volcano belching fish.

Bill, whenever I passed him, spoke in sentences which were precise and short. Once coming from the nets, his dogs charged directly at my team, almost as though they shared in the dissension which lay between us. They stopped dead in their tracks almost mouth to mouth with Whitey and Ginger who had bared their glistening teeth. That would have been a fight to see but we checked our dogs instantly. A few days later the same thing happened again and Bill apologized. As we went on, I realized that I did not care whose dogs attacked or what their owners thought. Torment and heartache had made me hard and I had little respect for beast and less for man.

Two Indians arrived from Caribou Point across the Lake to the east. They brought me meat and stimulated my desire to travel which had been growing stronger every week. The Fishery had become unbearable and I dreamed of hitching the dogs and going off for good. I had learned that Bill was taking his family to the Fort for Easter to celebrate Hib's marriage to Cecille. When he told me he said that he had promised to help me and would do so however he could, but did not wish my company.

I felt sorry for him in the days that followed when I would see him driving by with a load of wood, his face drawn and his voice tense with irritation. Once I heard him shouting angrily at his son, a pregnant change in one of gentle manners.

One afternoon I put my team in harness and set out along the north shore, running for several hours following the trail my friends from Caribou Point had left behind them. When I turned around, the sun was sinking beyond the western hills leaving a sky of blazing flame.

I stopped and talked to Celine when I reached her house already full of visitors. Pierre after greeting me pleasantly enough continued sawing wood. Without emotion, I began to reflect on the human mechanism by which men socially repudiate their neighbors. They offer just enough in formal gestures to block attack and cut each root of fresh affection before it bears a flower.

Some of the men had come back from a caribou hunt and, having killed five, offered me a shoulder which I went with them to get. One of the men's children was seriously ill and a quiet spread around his cabin which I could notice as we passed. No vestige of the sun remained when I reached home but the Northern Lights whirled like purple giants chasing orange balls around the sky. After I had fed my dogs, I could hear others baying in the distance, a sure sign, the Indians say, that someone soon will die.

On my birthday, I opened the third of my five cans of fruit for lunch having shared two in former celebrations. To my surprise, I found that this delicacy had lost much of its appeal. Nonetheless, I enjoyed the anniversary and would have marked it as a perfect day but for having broken off a molar tooth in biting hard on a splinter of caribou bone.

Bill was worried that Indians from the Dogrib band might come to trade while he was away so I offered to look after the store. He made a list of prices, becoming congenial as he worked. A few days later my feeling was relief when I saw the stretched line of toboggans cross the lake—Bill, Pierre, eight Indian men and all of their families trudging in groups between the sleighs.

The peaceful Fishery calmed my mind and then as though to match my mood, the lengthening days turned warm. One noon the thermometer rose above the melting point and my eyes pained from the sparkling snow spread out like a white plate of molten metal. On that night the temperature dropped over sixty degrees, but only to come up smiling in the morning.

One of the young men arrived for sugar and afterwards helped me move a net. He was a cheerful boy who sang and liked the girls or perhaps it was just the touch of spring. I returned to the settlement with him to visit a child of six who was dying of tuberculosis. The house was filthy and the air was hot and loathsome. While I condoled with the parents, a baby sister was trying to feed a needle to a boy of three. Sitting in a corner an old man carved a piece of a snowshoe frame, slowly pulling on a drawknife with a blade made from an old file and periodically holding the wood up toward the window to eye its thickness. When I got up to go, the sick girl turned her head and smiled.

On Easter morning I was called to the store for baking powder and tallow. All day long I could hear the drums for they were dancing across the bay. I started *Ann Veronica* and read intermittently throughout the night, wondering between times what it would be like to see London once more or talk to a woman in a Patou gown.

April came with a strong northwest wind and a flurry of snow. Indians came "to see store" and afterwards home with me for tea. I gave my singing friend a carton of matches to visit Bill's nets and he returned with three or four girls whom he had picked up along the way. He was wearing moccasins over heavy knotty stockings of blue and red his mother had knitted. His face was shiny from a thin coat of vaseline with which he had also combed his black hair into a glistening pompadour.

"Be-ke-kle—grease on him," one of the girls said giggling.

The others laughed for in the Indian idiom the expression means "he is good-looking" a reflection of the great prestige of oil or grease in the culture just as water denoted the opposite value. "Be-ke-tu—water on him," they would say of a poor or unattractive hunter.

As we joked, shyly glancing from one to another, two more men and an old woman came in, one bringing me a drum for which I had expressed a desire. The girls gave up their cups and I passed the tea. The old lady chattered away completely at her ease, only stopping to produce a short-stemmed pipe and ask me for tobacco which made the others laugh. When I gave it to her she convulsed the girls by the statement that now I had become her only sweetheart. Her old face, gnarled like spruce root, wrinkled up the faint lines tattooed in blue upon her chin, and her eyes twinkled with thoughts of years gone by. I gave her a spool of thread and said she would have to make me moccasins so that I could go hunting in the spring. She nodded her head and moaned softly, as though a price in labor had always been the burden of her joys.

The old man said that someone had shot a wolf and consequently would not use the gun again. The same fear set apart the wolverine as well and I heard of a hunter who caught one in his traps but gave the pelt away. These animals were powerful medicine and it behooved a wise man to treat them with respect. The conversation turned to the prowess of native doctors, shamans who performed miraculous acts like diving under the ice while the people watched, until wearily returning home they found the magician sitting by his stove.

While I listened, leaning on my table twisting a file between my hands, I noticed an open knothole in the surface of the boards. Covering one end of the tool in my fist over the aperture, I announced with impetuous caprice that I also was a medicine man. When all were watching, I opened my mouth and placing it over the upturned end of the file, proceeded to force its point inside me, gargling strangely as I worked my head closer to the table, while with my hidden hand I slowly drew the metal implement down through the knothole. The girls, screaming as they fell over each other in the attempt to reach the door, so startled me that I dropped the file. The others relieved by seeing it once again, still looked so fearful that I became constrained to show them how the trick was done, notwithstanding which I had the feeling that the older people reasoned that if I could swallow a file, I could just as suddenly create a knothole in my table.

To divert their thoughts I took the drum and warming its parchment head, began to copy the actions of a musician at the dances who was known for his ostentatious gesturing. This they loved for mimicry was cherished in their culture, and the old woman rocked on the floor with laughter. After I sat down exhausted, they nodded ther heads approvingly and when I had passed the tobacco once again, they all went home.

That night after my supper was over and I had fed the dogs, Peter came in the cabin sniffing from place to place in the brush, his nose pulsating with a sound like a heavy-duty engine turning over at full speed. He would only wrinkle his nostrils when a white man approached over the horizon, but Indians disturbed his peace of mind.

I was trading a mink at the store with some of the Dogrib band from the southeast section of the Lake when a boy ran in to say that he could see the people coming from the Fort. We went out to greet the weary travelers. Bill brought me mail that an airplane had dropped at the post and said the trip had been a hard one, with the children to safeguard from the cold.

In other ways he seemed refreshed from the change in scene and when I told him I was leaving shortly, he said the Father had missed me and invited me to stay with him again.

After I went to my shack, Bill's children came to see me and I fed them cocoa while they told me of their trip, still too excited to settle down at home. Little Rose's happy, smiling face lingered in my mind all evening as I sat on my bed listening to the music of the saws, chiming in the wind against a cabin wall.

27

THE day after the travelers returned, I pulled my nets, half reluctant at this parting symbol and half elated at the thought that the bitter task of visiting them was over. I went to say good-bye to Pierre who greeted me with pleasure and insisted that I stay to supper. We talked vaguely about the winter's troubles which he laughed off and blamed on women, saying they talked too much, and how the female gossip had ascribed my coming to his house as Celine's attraction.

"And so perhaps it was," I answered, "I would rather live with her than you."

This reaction warmed the Frenchman's heart and he began

to elaborate on the deprivations of my being all alone until once again emotion shook him. When I left for home, he offered to buy my nets and I promised them to him when I would be sure my need was over.

With Bill I discussed my future plans, stating that I might not return at all if there was a chance to reach the Yukon. If not, I would come back and visit the Indian bands spread out around the Lake. He gave me invaluable advice and offered me his Eskimo sled in case I wished to return and travel on the ice. When he said good night I realized that our relationship was cordial, but not intimate, and that I was still alone.

Before the evening sun went down I cut the hair between the toes of all the dogs, each holding up his paws patiently as though they knew that this would keep soft snow from freezing into icy balls which hurt their feet. Then I loaded my toboggan and went to bed.

The sun had not penetrated the heavy mist of early morning when I slid out of my eider down and pushed a few sticks into the stove. Enjoying the luxury of a last few minutes' doze while a little heat spread itself around the cabin, I wondered where I would camp that night. Looking through my window, I could see the slender silver ribbon of my chimney smoke crawling over snowdrifts to the west.

Putting on my clothes, I went outside to hitch the dogs. They seemed to know that we were going further than the woodpile and Scotty tried to pretend that he was still asleep so I dragged him quite unprotesting to the harness by the tail. When I had snapped him in the traces he promptly lay down for a final nap while I returned to the shack for a cup of cocoa.

We set off following the fish-net trail but had not crossed the bay before I tired of running and sat down on the load to smoke a cigarette, the dogs not slowing their quick step on the glassy surface of the Lake. Not a soul had been in sight as I left the Fishery but before we arrived at the south shore I could see blue curls wreathing above the Indian houses.

Peter tried to turn off to the fish nets but after I had yelled twice he gave up hope and continued on our way. Despite my previous experience on the flats, I missed the proper road and did not know it until we reached the bush. Again I lost almost an hour breaking trail toward the river through soft snow, the toboggan sometimes jamming in the trees, no easy matter to pull loose when weighed down with a heavy load.

When we returned to the hard path, we fairly sailed along, enough snow having blown in to fill the places where Indian sleighs from the Fort had fallen off. Although the trail was hard, the banks of snow on each side, already subsided to a few inches above the bottom of the toboggan, were very soft and formed a trap for the careless driver. Fortunately, Bill had warned me to keep my load well forward so that a smart steer dog like Ginger, even on the curves, could hold the toboggan from sliding off. On the icy surface my oak boards had gained the advantage held by birch on the salty stuff of midwinter, and we sped along with effortless grace.

Trees that had looked alike before now stood out in the bright sun to welcome us as familiar faces a hundred yards ahead. Before I knew it we were among the big poplars that marked the approach to Porcupine River and easing over the bank dashed down along the Bear. From the top of the steep pitch which once had cost me a pair of snowshoes I looked back to see bordering the farther shore, a blue vein of water belying its beauty with treacherous intent.

We pushed on across rolling country, relieved from monotony by a few small sloughs, until we rose to the higher land bordering Little River which drains the long stretch of muskeg between it and the mountains to the west. Coming to the stream, I saw the dogs point up their ears, telling me people were ahead and then I saw smoke curling out of the trees beyond the further bank.

When we arrived I found five toboggans with men and women eating their meal in the warmth of the fire, the last of the Easter visitors returning from the Fort. Each smiled or laughed in greeting and old Ereya with his long silvered hair came and shook my hand, warning me in slow and measured words like a father to his son that I should not be traveling alone through the forest. I loved the old man for his gentle courtesy and leaning a fish against the fire to roast sat down with him to share his tea. He reached for his smoke-blackened lard pail with a stick and filled my cup. I gave him tobacco in return and when I told him the drink was my first since I left the Lake, he showed surprise that I could have come so far without stopping to make a fire.

After the Indians had gone, I lay on my back with a cigarette and listened to the fading cries with which the people urged their ill-fed animals slowly homeward. Then I set off in the direction from which they had come, running lightly on the hard trail left behind them until we reached the ten-mile muskeg. As we moved across, I remembered how I had suffered on this stretch before, plunging on through the night, conscious only of my misery. Now setting our own pace and resting ten minutes in every hour, we moved like clockwork closer to the hills, but by the time we struck the halfway camp, the dogs and I were tired. I walked around looking at the spruce brush beds, frozen remnants of winter journeys, too cold to use again. It was a dismal spot, serving as an oasis for the weary but lacking beauty or protection from the open sweep of winds. The dogs looked strong, and, picking up the headline I decided to leave this monotonous land of brush and sticks behind.

Near sunset, some bushy spruce among the white poles caught my eye, and stopping, I set about my preparations for the night with such a leisureliness that it brought a pleasant consciousness of my own certainty and skill. I fried some moosemeat and turn the dogs loose to choose their beds. Peter sat near by, watching me eat my supper while his frozen fish warmed and sagged against a smoking log.

Then I called the others and they came, sitting in a semicircle while I threw the limp silver morsels, one after another, into the open mouths. Lying in my sleeping bag I looked through the branchless long-dead trees at stars so thick they made one conscious of the intervening shapes of grayish blue.

"How beautiful," I said to Peter, "we should have run away long months ago."

Then I heard a whistle from the fire and an answering voice which whispered "I told you to."

Surprised, I raised my head. In the scarlet glow of velvet coals I saw her sitting beside the fire, her long hair like birch leaves in the autumn spilling down over her white fox coat. She kicked a twig of brush with a foot no longer than an ermine from which her boots were made and watched me from the corner of her eyes.

"Don't your knees get cold?" I said, fascinated by the curves of skin which disappeared beneath her parka.

"Never mind my legs," she answered with a laugh like snow which suddenly slips down a mountain slope in spring. "Go to sleep so you will love the woods tomorrow."

"Come closer then," I said. She moved beside my bed, and breathing heavily I seemed to see twin stars like sparkling studs of ice flashing and twinkling in the bosom of the sky.

The sun had not risen when I awoke and built the fire, melting the snow water left in the tea pail from the night before. I sipped three cups of cocoa before harnessing the dogs and then as the first rays of light reflected on the treetops, I loaded the sleigh and drove off toward the pass, climbing slowly up the slope of Eta-de-nat-le. This morning, however, the ridge renounced its name for instead of being dark, it was dripping with gold as the little balls of mist melted from the tamaracks.

We stopped in the grove of birch which marks the crest and then raced down onto Poor Fish Lake in less than an hour and a half so that I was glad to sit on the load while we crossed it, throwing back my hood and taking off my mittens to cool my heated body.

After another stretch only slightly longer, I was snubbing the toboggan over the edge of Steep Bank River and speeding toward Loon Lake. The toboggan whistled in its silver groove and as I ran laughing I yelled playfully, "Hurry up, Neidja, or you'll be left behind." When I jumped onto the sleigh for the twenty-minute crossing, she sat beside me twirling a twig of spruce in my face like spray from snow in the wind.

We had lunch on the western shore and Neidja spilled the tea pail when I told her to let me eat, so I rubbed her face with snow and she ran off into the timber.

The sun was low on the horizon before our journey was over. The trail had been broken to pieces and the toboggan continually dipped and swerved almost throwing the tired dogs from their feet. Twenty lakes we passed until finally I could see the black outline of Bear Rock loom up larger and larger from the Mackenzie shore, blotting out the colors of the distant sunset. Then with a long dive through the willows, we came out on the winding road into the settlement and pulled up in front of the mission door.

The Father gave me a genial greeting and showed me the unused kennels behind the church. With sudden exuberant energy, Whitey jumped on top of his doghouse and lifted a weary leg toward the swiftly rising moon.

28

THE Father's house was large and had been built soon after 1876 when the Mission had been founded. It was a two-story building with one large room in the center still used for services during the winter. To the left was a combination kitchen and dining room with a table against the wall, to the right several smaller rooms in an equivalent space, one serving for the post office and the others as bedrooms. The Father gave me the commodious quarters on the second floor above the main hall, and after washing, I came down to dinner.

When a steaming bowl of food had been placed on the table, the Father speedily said the gratitude, holding his battered tweed cap a few inches off his head, then slapped it on again, and sat down, his pink cheeks smiling through his heavy silver beard.

"You take a great risk traveling alone," he said, ladling out a large dish of the hot soup and passing it to me.

"I like to, Father," I answered. "It is much easier to drive dogs when there is no one in front to slow you down and no one pushing from behind. You have to take the responsibility for everything that happens but you don't get angry for a partner's failures. Actually one's own mistakes hurt most from hurting others. Then also the forest is strangely beautiful in its solitude when one learns to know it. I love the sun breaking through the trees and the million stars which gently dance at night."

He laughed softly. "You see a lot for one who drives so fast."

"It is the dogs that have the speed. There is no team like them." The emphasis with which I responded came from an unconscious wish to change the subject. "Forgive me Father, I do not want to boast. I simply mean that these dogs pull hour after hour with all their strength where others would lack the will."

"Yes I have heard it is true. The animals are very fine, but what will happen if you sprain an ankle and no one is there to help? You could not handle a toboggan very long without two good legs on which to stand."

"That's a risk I choose to take. After all, there are more important things to think about."

"Perhaps you are right, my son. Now eat your food before it cools."

The taste was like nothing I had ever put into my mouth before: cabbage from the Father's garden boiled in a broth of moosemeat with a little rice and oatmeal, then spices, and finally a few floes of bread on top.

"The meal is marvelous, Father. One touch of France can turn plain food into a gift from heaven."

"I am glad you appreciate *garbure*. My mother made it so when I was a boy but perhaps I have improved it just a little—who knows?" The Father chuckled in his beard. "When you leave, I shall give you a few frozen cabbages for the sleigh and you can try yourself."

After we had finished eating, the Father wiped his knife and fork on his napkin and rolled them in it, whereupon I did the same. Then he took his usual seat in the big hall by the window, throwing a heavy shawl over the skirt of his worn black cassock as I drew up a chair beside him. We talked of things one wants to know to take the measure of a man and discover if the cloth of friendship fits, where the pockets of admiration and respect are sewn, and where the seams. At last with mutual affection he sent me off to bed, weary and heavy with food.

I awakened to the mumbling of the Mass resounding against the boards beneath my head. Dressing quickly to the sound of the Kyrie eleison, I went down and joined the four or five women bowed among the benches. The Father looked majestic in a chasuble of violet, the iridescent silk catching the golden gleam of the orphrey threads, while in a sweet strong voice he chanted the canon prayers.

After breakfast I went to the Hudson's Bay Company. Mac jumped up with such great enthusiasm in his greeting that I was touched and pleased. He wanted to know everything that had happened and we talked avidly for an hour about the life and customs at the Lake. When our conversation shifted to the local scene, Mac's face turned dour and as I mentioned his compatriots in the village he only answered "I haven't seen them" or "How would I know?" Then I sat and listened to the strains of the "Habanera" which his ruddy-cheeked Scotch assistant was playing on the gramophone, at last departing for the village, thinking that Mac was really queer.

When my next acquaintance boomed a welcome my confidence in sanity returned but after the amenities were passed, I noticed the same taciturn resentment of others in the town, as though some smouldering animosity burned within which needed only a puff of words to fill the throat's flue with spleenful bitterness. In each house it was the same except for variations of restraint in verbal acrimony. To me, however, they were kind and promised presents when I left.

That night after dinner I told the Father of my experience and his face saddened.

"It is always so at this time of the year. In another month I shall hear the angry arguments even at my door and will count it well if none resorts to physical violence. Then when the boat comes down in July, they will drink and wear off their malice but by the time next year's cabbages are grown, they will all be on good terms again. Perhaps that is why I like the fall."

We went on talking. The Father asked me about the famous evolution trial which still sent out reverberations beyond the frontiers of easy communication. Smiling, I told him that government administrators had warned me not to stir the ire of the priests by raising controversial issues, and he chuckled merrily. For an hour I outlined the development of evolution hypotheses from Darwin on, the old man nodding his head and interpolating questions from time to time. When I had concluded with an apology for being captivated by my own enthusiasm, he said that he could not remember having had such a stimulating conversation, which made me understand one price he had paid for his forty years among the Indians.

I told him that I planned to leave in the morning with Johnny O and four other mountain men who had arrived the day before after almost a week of breaking trail from the west. They said it was possible that I might still be able to reach the Yukon but would be glad to have me come with them in any case. Others in the village had warned me that the trip was dangerous but I had shrugged my shoulders, knowing that they seldom left the Fort and considered the whole environment a menace. The Father showed his concern in more than words, however, as he told me how the snows melted on the mountain slopes long before the sun's heat warmed the lowlands, sending streams of water down on the river ice which, when it froze, formed only an unsupporting crust, hard to distinguish and often circling around to trap the unsuspecting traveler. Once the Bear Lake bands had tried the western trip but lost their dogs and had not ventured since. When I promised to be careful we let the subject drop. Where Johnny and his friends could go, so might I, I thought.

The Father asked me if I did not fear to die and I answered that I was afraid but not of being dead. The issue had been settled in my mind, I claimed, admitting that if his belief was true I would find myself in Hell. My host laughed lightly and I challenged him to prove me wrong. For hours we fenced with theology and scripture as I showed that neither innocence nor ignorance was on my side. Late into the night this strange argument continued, the Father kind and unbelieving, until weary with the effort he rose to go to bed saying, "Oof, maybe, maybe!" Then he turned with twinkling eyes and added, "But be careful in the mountains."

29

WHEN I awoke at six-thirty, I could see the Indians crossing the River with their toboggans loaded. I did not stop to eat, and harnessing my dogs with speed raced after them. I closed on their teams within a mile and we continued on about four more to a place where we climbed the bank. There they picked up dog-food caches and their snowshoes, which they had left like sentinels standing sternly in the snow.

Up through dense willows we wound our way until we reached an open tableland; then on through country marked by birch and rising ground around a mountainside. Where the forest was thick a road had been cut the like of which I had never seen and when we stopped for lunch old Hochile proudly boasted of it as his own. I nodded out of deference to his pride but knew this trail to be a relic of the days of Ninety-eight when throngs of gold-mad men had tried to open up a road to Dawson, dragging on sledges the iron stoves which still rust in the summer rains along the way.

After our hasty meal, I took the lead with Johnny O hard on my heels, running away from the others on the straightest trail in all the north, laid out with instrument precision like some leafy boulevard. All afternoon we climbed upwards toward the peaks. Johnny stopped me once to give a warning before we plunged precipitously into a hidden valley and I checked the momentum of the toboggan on the glasslike trail by dragging both feet in the edging snow. Even with this precaution, twice I had to stop to extricate the nearest dogs entirely buried by the sleigh. I worried for their safety but they clambered out unhurt. Once more we started on the upward rise, passing over a high ridge and turning slightly to the right to follow the winding steep slope of a little river valley for several hours and fringing cliffs where the Indians had felled big spruce to hold the road from sliding off. We began to see hills behind us and I wondered at the new experience of traveling with natives who raced from dawn to noon and went unstopping past the suppertime.

At eight-thirty we reached the camp they made while breaking trail, still two nights out from the River Fort. Johnny made the fire and Etchinlere filled a frying pan with grease, waiting until it melted before he took it off to sprinkle it with pounded meat and sugar which with a sizzle sucked in the liquid oil. I contributed Bear Lake whitefish only to discover that this food for them was a rare delicacy which they preferred to meat.

Then we crowded down on the bed of brush before the fire, each curled up like a dog in blankets, I still resisting slumber. Old Hochile next to me had taken a final pinch of snuff and periodically released a stream of liquid straight up into the air for the wind to distribute according to the laws of chance. I accepted this Indian custom but when as I was on the verge of sleep, he drenched me below one eye, I cautiously reached out and gave his face a shove. He rolled part way over with a grunt and I covered up my head and slept.

The fire was burning when I wakened at four-thirty to see a chilly fog floating down from a near-by mountain peak. I stretched myself close to the flames, looking half maliciously at Hochile while I pulled on my boots. Johnny O and I allowed the others to go ahead while we finished our tea and then set out after them passing all the toboggans at the first spell. Our pace had slowed as we climbed at a sharper angle for a second hour and Scotty ever fighting for a leading distance pulled out two claws as he struggled up the icy slopes.

About nine o'clock we turned onto the course of a narrow mountain stream, following it as we wound through the hills. The white peaks ahead seemed very close and soft clouds spread out over the valley behind us. Johnny O had shifted to the lead and I saw him snatching glances at black splotches on the farther bank where the sun was lighting up the snow. Then I realized the reason for our speed.

Johnny stopped and I walked around my team to find out what he thought. He pointed across the gorge and I saw patches of loose mud from which small rivulets of water were disappearing beneath the snow.

"That means water on the Gravel River. We can make it to our camp but we can't use toboggans in the mountains any more this year."

The others drew up behind us and nodded in affirmation. My heart sank as I looked around at the clean white snow that I had come to love. Suddenly I heard a whistle in the evergreens and caught a glimpse of Neidja laughing and pointing toward the east.

"Johnny, I can race the water down the valley over such a perfect trail and still reach the Barren Ground plateau before the spring!"

"Sure, I think so," he answered. "Just beyond our night camp you will find no water for a month and the Big Lake—well, you know there is no summer there."

With a sense of sorrow at our parting, I shook the hand of each new friend and gave him fish, receiving in turn dried slabs of caribou or moose. Old Hochile, with a speech, presented a bag of pounded meat and a block of frozen bear fat to feed me on my journey. I turned the dogs around and with a final wave, whirled down the stream, watching anxious-eyed the dirty splotches on the bank.

By early afternoon, having passed through water only once, I reached the place where we had slept and after cooking lunch began winding down through the lower hills, most of the time dragging my feet to hold the toboggan off the dogs. Then with a turn around a canyon entrance we stopped breathless at the view of an endless valley stretched out below, with the trail running like a taut string toward the River. For the first time during the winter, I had an uninterrupted ride, leaning easily on the load while the dogs trotted hour after hour, scarcely conscious of the toboggan as it whirred down the silver chute, leaving the mountains to melt away in darkness before the dying sun. Neidja ran beside me, sometimes jumping on in front and throwing snowballs at Peter when he slowed his pace to lap up moisture on his hanging tongue.

When we shot among the willows, I hugged the sleeping bag spread on top of the load and for thirty minutes dared not raise my head as the dogs raced through the wicker funnel, my shoulders stinging from the whip of branches as they sprang back across the sleigh. The River was desolate in the moonlight as we followed along the bank, picking our way over jagged reefs of ice finally to turn across and climb to the Mission yard.

The Father had kept a lantern burning and welcomed me with smiles.

"I shall sleep more comfortably, now that you have returned." There was a slight note of exasperation in his voice. "It is better if you wander to stay in country that you know. After Easter those mountains are a dangerous place for anyone to travel. And now good night."

In the morning, the Father gave me cabbages and also soup,

frozen in a kettle and then knocked out and cut with an ax into blocks, which only needed melting in a little boiling water to be transmuted into what it was before. I loaded the toboggan with corn meal and tallow for the dogs while some of my village friends came to say good-bye, each unceremoniously bringing some contribution for my welfare such as a loaf of bread or a bag of sugared cakes. The Corporal presented me with a roll of magazines less than a year old, a prize indeed and when I asked how he acquired such treasure, knowing the mail sled delivered only first-class letters, he said an airplane had brought them, the first to land in winter at this northern post. He pointed out an open expanse of river snow beyond the village near the place where the trail led off to the Lake. I could barely make out the faint traces left by heavy skiis. "It was an experience for the people," the Father said. "You would have been impressed to see old Kagaye nodding his head and repeating 'Mola di-e, mola di-e—white man, this is too much!' "

The men admired my dogs and told me that Pierre had said the leader had such great intelligence that he could write his name. Some smiled and one more brash said that he knew of a smarter dog.

"Watch and perhaps he will show you something," I answered him and, yelling to the team, shoved off toward the River. We picked our way along to the open sheet of wind-blown snow. There I jumped on the toboggan and called to my mongrel bull. Straight he went for a hundred feet and then as I signalled he swung sharply to the right and in a perfect semicircle returned to the middle of the course and followed it back; another command and he began a tight loop, then a long narrow leaf-shaped one, and so continued until we left a trail along the top to cross a *T*. Pulling up the bank onto the eastern road, we waved farewell. Out on the River the deep imprint of the toboggan spelled out "Peter" for all the world to see.

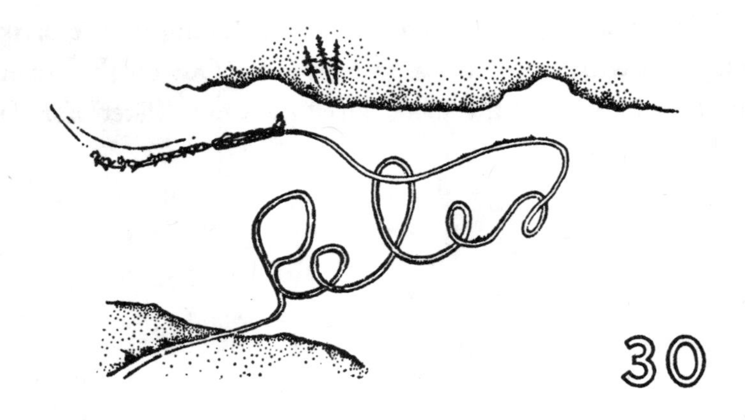

30

THE return to the Fishery had been accomplished without serious difficulties. My greeting was mild but Bill, when I told him that I expected to leave as soon as possible to go around the Lake, proceeded to outline what information he thought would be helpful.

He hauled over his Eskimo sled which had runners twelve feet long shod with flat strips of iron as a protection against the ice. I decided that I could fasten my small tin stove permanently between the runners in the front where there were no crossbars and then put a solid box at the back, leaving only a step behind. In between the two would be enough room to stretch out my eider down to provide a place to sleep off the ground if it should be damp. When desirable, I could pitch my tent over the whole sled and have my traveling camp inside. The stove was a necessity as there was little wood around the Barrens and naturally none at all on the ice over which I expected to make long crossings.

Bill had picked up his traps while I was gone, catching three marten, a white fox, and a beautiful silver, but one of his little girls had ruined the foxes in the warehouse, singeing them with a candle. Quite apart from this incident, he seemed depressed, almost morose at times. His wife gave me a moose nose, having heard of my early interest, since turned into a joke.

The weather had become mild with the temperature rising in midday well above freezing, but then it would drop fast in the evening, fifty or sixty degrees of variation not being uncommon. Traveling henceforth would be at night, for the dogs could not stand working in the midday sun, overheated by their heavy coats of fur. Actually, it made little difference otherwise for, including dusk and dawn, there were only a few hours of starlight.

The dogs would need shoes to protect their feet on bare ice and, with Bill's advice, I arranged to have Takazo sew me all she could from ten yards of cotton duck. She must have paid herself liberally with the material or perhaps just wearied herself from the monotony of the labor for she returned with only seventy-nine. We joked the matter off, and she went back with more cloth as well as a piece of tanned mooseskin from which she promised five pairs of moccasins for me. I was ready to depart but I could not leave without the necessary footwear.

When I went to speed her efforts I visited the sick girl who was lying unconscious with two women on each side smoking and spitting in a can. Two old men sat on a trunk near the head of the bed, also smoking, and looking very serious. At her feet, a pair of candles burned. Other people came in, some to moan softly and others seemingly indifferent to the common tragedy. That night the child died and the next day I could hear the drums beating for the death dance while a snow fell steadily over the village.

Pierre came to call on me bringing clothes. He wanted my nets and offered to give me two bales of whitefish that his wife had dried. I accepted the exchange quickly as the bundles, which weighed only one third the amount of an equivalent number of green fish, would provide a needed margin of safety in calculating dog food for my trip. They stayed for supper which I discovered to my surprise I had learned to prepare creditably. The subject of moose nose inevitably was broached and I told Celine that I had been boiling one for two days but still could not chew it. When I showed it to her, she immediately began to eat, laughing and saying my teeth were poor.

We talked of fur and Pierre offered to show me his catch while Celine smiled. I told him that when an Indian had brought me a mink to trade at the store while they were gone at Easter, I had been so excited that I could not tell it from a marten. Celine smiled at this admission and began to list distinctions—the texture of the hair and how the mink fur was whiter at the throat and the marten ivory, sometimes blending into yellow. These things I knew but I lacked certainty of mind when I had to decide alone. Then she told me when one blows the hair, there is color to the skin beneath; how this changes in the mink from white in summer to black in autumn and then turns lighter as the pelt grows prime. I promised to remember and she said that she would take me trapping with her in the fall. I gave her a French embroidered handkerchief that had belonged to a friend of mine and she sat quietly looking at it for a long time.

When they had gone I left my door wide open to clear the smoke and Peter came in and sniffed around. I asked him whether he would like to take another trip and he shrugged his shoulders and curled up on the brush licking a paw still sore from mountain climbing.

One afternoon as I was checking over my possessions an Indian woman came into my cabin. She took tobacco that I offered but would not speak beyond her greeting. When I asked her why she came, she answered, "E-ku-ri," and sat silently against the wall with her head hung down.

She was middle-aged, a woman widowed in the summer who had remarried while at the Fort on Easter. I could see that she was troubled but knowing the people's ways, I left her to her sorrows and went about my business.

After a little while her husband arrived and taking some tobacco hunched down beside her. She leaned away but did not raise her face and neither spoke a word. A little later as I counted the cartridges remaining for my gun I became conscious of their voices, first soft and hesitant, then antagonistic, and finally rising to the pitch of heat where I forgot my calculations.

"For Christ's sake, either shut up," I said, "or tell me what's the matter!"

They did not understand the words but felt the meaning. Both began to talk at once and after I had quieted them again, the husband spoke.

"She will not take a bath!"

This strange accusation struck me in the ribs and I laughed until I toppled off my box with tears running from my eyes.

"What was it you said?" I queried.

"My wife, she won't take a bath."

They both looked at me as though I were a judge to whom they had imparted some fearful confession of great significance.

"Is that bad?" I asked.

Then the husband started on a long monologue from which I gathered that the priest had once given a sermon on the need for cleanliness and he wanted me to substantiate the statement that all white women bathed.

His wife looked at him fixedly while he talked. Then she turned to me and said, "I no take bath for first husband; I no take bath for him!"

Feeling the seriousness of my role I explained that while it was true that women in my country bathed, I had never heard of a widow who bathed for her second husband if she had not done so for her first. I added with final emphasis that I believed it even might be dangerous.

They pondered on my answer, comparing thoughts they had. Then both thanked me for my wisdom and walked off peacefully toward their home.

The weather turned cold, and then mild again, but the wind kept blowing. I bought some smoked glasses at the store which were easier on my eyes than the green pair I sometimes used. Bill had warned me that if I had one bad attack of snow blindness while I traveled alone, I might as well put a bullet in my head. Warmhearted Pierre had told me to be sure to shoot my dogs beforehand as he could not stand the thought of wolves cutting down a team like mine.

I turned in all my extra supplies and went to see two Indians of the Dogrib band who had come in for shells. They were good-natured men and I told them as they left that I might see them at their camp. Then I worked on the sled and harness, testing each lashing and strap. The next day I loaded carefully, at the last moment remembering to buy some four-inch trout hooks, and at ten o'clock that night I said good-bye to Bill.

31

AS SOON as we were out on the open Lake I sat down on the box at the back of the sled, which though heavy the dogs pulled with ease on the smooth surface of the hard Lake snow. I watched the cabins of the settlement recede as the last glow of the sun left the gray outline of a ghost town at the edge of the bay. Peter sniffed occasionally for the trail that had been made by the Dogrib men but had no difficulty in following it.

For the first hour I was intrigued by the sensations of my new experience, so different from traveling with snowshoes and toboggan. The smoothness of the ride resulting from the weight and length of the sled made me feel as though I were sitting on the open platform of an observation car while the train pulled out on the main line in the dead of a winter night. Even the intermittent knobs of ice that thumped the load turned for the moment into switches over which the car wheels rolled, clicking through the dark.

The lack of the appendages on my feet, which through months of use had become almost a part of my limbs, was like an amputation and I wiggled my toes as a country boy does in spring when he first discards his shoes. It seemed so simple to step on and off the sled and with the end of my eider down as a cushion, I sat cross-legged on the box gazing at the sky line of the Fish Mountains beyond the northern shore. The dogs showed no effort in their running so I decided to rest them only fifteen minutes each two hours. As the darkness drifted down, my body chilled and I jumped off the sled to run behind. Here and there I could dimly make out mounds of snow and ice and shortly after midnight I saw in the distance a blurred peninsula of trees jutting out offshore. On we trotted, the dogs with heads down, their haunches rolling slightly from side to side with the steady beat of thumping paws.

It seemed a longer time than I had guessed when we stopped to take our ease a hundred yards out from the end of Whiskey-jack Point. I gave each dog a pat and checked their feet. All were in good condition and I sat down looking at the shore and wondered whether the Indians named this landmark because of the number of birds or whether when clearly seen, it showed a crest like the Canada jay.

Rounding the point, our road shifted to the northeast and

we ran toward Low Sand Point, some fifteen miles away. A light snow began to fall and now and then we lost the trail, always to pick it up again when it bared itself within range of Peter's nose. Actually the sled ran smoother when we made our own trail for the Indian dogs had veered from side to side while Peter held a truer course.

At dawn we hit a pressure ridge but climbed through it with a minimum of difficulty as the natives had found a cleft only a few feet high. I could remember the thunder coming off the Lake when the ice, expanding with great pressure, heaved to throw up such jagged dikes with a grinding, crunching roar. Now the process would be reversed. Without the terror of the noise,. the lightning stab of cracking ice would strike, splitting the frosted surface to leave a dangerous snake of jade-green water through which the dogs might fall. With the thought of such a chance, I looked at the solid runners of the sled and they somehow seemed less long.

The sun was shining brightly when we reached the further point at four o'clock and pulled up on the shore. Wood was scarce but I made a little fire and freed the dogs who were still in a mood to smell around, but soon returned to curl up near my open bed of boughs.

It was early afternoon when I awoke and cooked a meal of moosemeat, giving half-frozen whitefish to the dogs. We walked along the shore to take our bearings, my four friends frolicking in the low bushes but never running out of sight. Having satisfied our curiosity we returned and I lay down to read behind a stump, comfortably warmed by the sun in my protected nook, while the dogs dozed lazily near by.

After tea I harnessed up at eight in preparation for the traverse due east across the second largest of the five great bays which taken all together comprise the whole of Great Bear Lake.

The Indian trail showed up clearly but swerved so frequently that I seldom knew in which direction we were heading. As far as I could see there lay only an endless expanse of ice and snow. The dogs ran briskly but a piercing wind blew from the north and prevented my riding except for a few minutes at a time. The team made a peculiar picture, with hair frosted a pure silver on the protected side, the line of color sharply showing down the middle.

At the first rest period I found Scotty's forepaws getting raw and also one of Peter's so I slipped their feet in little canvas bags. Scotty seemed to welcome the protection, licking my hands as I doubled the strings around above the dewclaw and tied them with a slipknot. Peter put up his foot as I requested but when I said "What is the matter, fellow?" he closed his eyes slowly like someone who would prefer to forget the whole affair.

On into the night we went, hour after hour. I saw a cliff of snow rising up in the distance and while I was wondering how we could have come to shore so soon, we suddenly veered by this promontory which proved to be a four-foot pile of ice that had been thrown into false perspective by mists that presage the dawn. Gradually we could discern a pale yellow light on the far horizon turning into pink while the morning fog closed in. I felt a damp kiss on my cheek and there was Neidja skipping along beside me.

"Where have you been?" I asked her in an almost hungry voice.

"I have been chasing rainbows," she answered, as though I should have known that it was a natural thing to do.

"But there are no rainbows," I said, looking all around.

"Silly!" she whispered, her eyes twinkling as she took my hand, "How could there be when I have driven them all away."

"I think them beautiful," I teased, and she snatched her fingers out from mine. "Not half so lovely as you," I added, suddenly aware that she wore a baby rabbitskin bolero that hung open at the front.

"You would not like it if the rain were to come while you make this crossing. Water is a million times more dangerous than cold," and with the thought she seemed to fade away.

"Wait," I cried, "don't leave me all alone!"

Then she came very close when I stopped and for a minute I held her in my arms, her cool face pressed tight to mine.

"Perhaps one day I shall never leave you," she whispered in my ear. Then she kissed me on the cheek again and disappeared.

I rubbed my face which was moist with fog and stretched my arms against the wind. Then I turned the dogshoes so that the thinning surfaces were on the top and yelled at Peter to move on. For several hours we ran until the sun climbed in the sky dispelling with its heat the slinking mist. In the distance I could see a range of hills that marked the southern shore. Almost imperceptibly we closed upon them, picking our way through roughening ice. My left knee began to pain and the dogs panted wearily with Scotty weaving in the harness—nearly at the limit of his strength. At eight o'clock the trees were clearly visible and Peter raised his head to smell the musky land, almost hopping in his interest to find the shortest route ashore. We crossed some open cracks about a foot in width and stopped to drink, then raced on, Peter veering onto the trail we had lost some miles before and dashing up an open slope pulled in beside the remnants of an Indian camp. Without bothering to build a fire, I crawled into my blankets, exhausted from the thirteen-hour crossing, and slept until the middle of the afternoon.

When I wakened I walked out on the point and climbed an ice ridge about fifteen feet in height. As far as I could see in any direction, there was no distinguishing feature except the endless flank of Bear Mountain stretched out prone to the east in a white blanket flecked with sticks. To the southwest lay the flat and ill-defined shore of Kla-do-e—Great Bay—toward which I had looked so often from my cabin door.

Returning to the sled I built a fire and fed the dogs the last green fish. Then I fried some moosemeat and drank moss-flavored cocoa made with water from a little pool which had collected in a basin down among the rocks. The spot was pleasant rugged country with wind-swept clumps of gnarled and twisted spruce that set off scenic islands in the snow. The dogs were glad to rest, lying on their sides with legs and bellies toward the warming sun.

When we slid down off the shore that night I rode across a rim of slush, then turned northward along the mountain, persuading Peter to travel straight from point to point instead of following the trail of Indians whose dogs, through fear or habit, hugged the coast. I found that I had tied one of Scotty's shoes too tight so that it chafed his leg and then a half hour later lost it because the string had loosened. Once we found a crack so wide that Peter feared to jump but when I crossed ahead and called, he leaped before the sound had left my mouth.

For two nights we marched along beneath the mountain, once turning the sled bottom side up while sliding down from our tea camp on a jutting neck of land. The flexible lashings held the wooden pieces tight so all I had to do was to reload the things that tumbled out. On the second morning, several hours before the dawn, we watched Bear Mountain flatten out, and picking up the trail, followed it across the barren plain behind Red Point, dipping in and out of bays until we reached a little stream from which the snow had gone. Sliding over the glassy ice, we came suddenly on the Dogrib camp without a sound. Quietly I pitched the tent a hundred feet away.

32

IT WAS past noon when I awoke and walked up toward the largest tent with Whitey and Scotty flanking my sides while Ginger pressed at my heels and Peter stepped briskly out in front. Halfway to the center of the camp, a pack of mongrels charged down on us and I waited, tightening my hold on the doubled dog chain which I carried in my hand. Whitey and Ginger turned, raging in defiance and I jingled the steel links that I held. We were encircled by some thirty animals which in a moment had stopped dead in their tracks. An Indian stuck his head out of a tent flap but said nothing and as we started to walk again, I could feel Whitey's side pressed lightly against my leg. Whitey held his head high with clear disdain until an Indian dog came too close to suit him. Then he shot out his head with jaws distended in a ferocious growl and when that failed to intimidate the intruder he mocked a leap which terrified a dozen.

At the door, the Indian picked up a stick of wood and hurled it at the pack and then another with a yell. to send them running. My dogs lay down while I shook hands and stepped into the tent.

Beyond the stove six or seven men were sitting in the brush with a deck of cards before them. They opened up a place for me at the back and went on playing rummy while they asked me questions about the trail and what game I had seen. Several women came in to join those in front and one passed me a plate of boiled whitefish from the pail that simmered on the little stove.

They told me that food had been scarce until the last few weeks when the trout began to bite. Rabbits, which the Indians say decrease in a seven-year cycle, had been almost nonexistent, one old man protesting that never in his life had he seen so few. Also the caribou had shifted to the east and only a stray band had come their way. As he complained of the shortage of game, I recalled men who had watched the caribou pass for three days on end, crowding a valley gap a mile in width, and tales of how for years the Indians shot them down, taking only the tongues so that the whole Barrens smelled of rotting carcasses.

After we had talked and joked an hour, I walked back to my camp and built a fire on which to cook corn meal and tallow for the dogs in a gasoline can which I had carried for that purpose. When the mush had cooled somewhat, I poured it out in piles upon the snow. Ginger burned his tongue a little and walked around sucking away as though some gum had stuck to the roof of his mouth. Scotty did not like the change in fare but soon lapped up his yellow pile like all the rest.

Later in the evening I returned to the Indian tents and watched Alexi and Susi Tucho playing a game like checkers on a crudely carved board twenty squares deep with five rows of men to a side. They moved the pieces from the start as though each were a king to jump backwards and forwards at will. Then when a piece reached the opponent's king line, the player would jump over his own men in any diagonal move. When the game was over, Alexi invited me to supper in his tent near by. We dined on pounded meat dipped in bear grease with sugar sprinkled on the top, my favorite dish.

That night I could not sleep for a long time as I had grown accustomed to seeking my bed after dawn. The wind howled and some anomalous half fear held me. When I dressed and strolled outside, two girls came bringing a log but when I gave each a present they went away and returned with cut-up wood. Susi Tucho's wife walked with them carrying a gift of trout. I gave her a present also, together with some flour with which to make me bannock.

After I had eaten I sauntered out on the ice where the men were setting hooks at intervals along a two-foot crack. They had the ubiquitous willows, one to lay across the fissure and a second hooked piece that hung down into the water. For line they used a thirty-foot length of wrapping cord, one end fastened to the bottom of the crotched willow and the other to a large hook onto which a section of whitefish had been sewn in imitation of its young.

Alexi had just pulled out a three-foot monster and was re-setting by folding the line, except for the last two yards, into a little bow which he fastened at the end of the pole with a slipknot. Thus, he explained, when a trout struck, pulling the bow loose would set the hook in its mouth, and it would then swim away, hardly ever snapping the stretched out cord. When lucky, the men were catching several fish to a hook each day.

I spent the afternoon making a few sets of my own, walking back to camp in a fleecy snow that reminded me of the fall. I saw two geese pass over, honking as they went, and some men rushed out of their tents imitating the cry to call them back. The geese kept on, unswerving in their flight, and the men went in again, laughing among themselves.

The next day I pulled my hooks and caught two trout of which one was big and one was small. I gave the little fish, which weighed about fifteen pounds, to Scotty and he ate it all, licking the snow to catch the bloody drippings. The larger trout I cut into four pieces, one for each of the other dogs and one to make a block of steaks for me. Alexi came to visit and I presented him with a box of rifle cartridges which pleased him very much. He invited me to dinner and we shared a pail of boiled moosemeat with fish heads on the side. Then we played poker with the others for an hour until I broke up the game to load my sled. I did not collect my easy winnings but gave Alexi a bag of tea for which he returned a slab of moosemeat. The men all came down to help me pull my sled over the ridges onto the smooth ice. Then as I set my course around the point, they watched me go, standing immobile for several minutes, before walking back to camp.

That night I ran only a few hours down into the smallest of the Lake's five bays and with the break of dawn camped at the edge of rolling muskeg, happy to be alone.

When I left the following day, the sun was still shining and I sat on my box reading a magazine while the dogs trotted along contentedly over the unbroken snow. After dusk had fallen and I was straining my eyes to see the print, I suddenly felt the whole team lurch sidewise and begin to run. Startled, I twisted around in haste. The dogs had slowed their pace but each had his head turned and ears upraised, staring at the snow. Following their gaze I saw a wee mouse scampering toward the shore as fast as its little legs could run. With a deep breath of relief I laughed so loud the dogs twisted their heads over their shoulders to look at me.

"Go on, you babies!" I yelled, still shaking from the tension and its consequent release.

We followed our course due south, while every hour or so a flock of geese appeared in view to pass overhead squawking like Paris taxis. Toward morning a heavy mist closed in and, as it cleared, several gulls flew after us as though we were a ship, soaring back and forth across our wake.

That day I slept among the tamarack and birch which had

increased in number along the shore. The next night, leaving my tent behind me, I ran down past rocky islands to the narrow end of the bay where a little river, called "Tu-ri-le—Running Water" from a riffle near its mouth, flows out to feed the lake. The Tu-ri-le Indians apparently had crossed the portage to Kla-do-e to set their trout hooks, from which place they might safely reach the Fishery on the last ice of the year. At least I could not find their tracks and I retraced my steps in a drizzling rain that of a moment turned to hail. As I approached my camp I thought that I had never seen a lovelier sight than tamarack in frozen fog.

For another night I followed the gleaming twin lines of my sled trail northward. Bare patches were spreading along the bank and here and there the snow had turned to slush. I was still some miles from my former camp when I saw two men dragging fish across the ice at the opening of an inlet. They waved as I turned in. When we met they said they lived with Susi Tucho's father behind the point. I loaded the five big trout they had and drove them home as I wished to meet the old man who having grown feeble with the years, had not visited the Fort for many seasons.

A low fire burned beside a spread of spruce boughs with tall poles slanting up to an adjacent tree, each carrying huge flanks of several split trout glistening a bright orange in the sun. Twisting curls of smoke blew across their silver scales which crinkled as they dried. The aged veteran of the woods with long gray hair that parted in the middle stared at me with curious eyes and when his nephew told him who I was, he nodded very slowly and indicated a seat beside him, half moving over to denote his welcome. He asked the usual questions about the place from which I had come and what signs of game I had seen in passing but I think his words were spoken more out of courtesy or custom than any need, for I had the feeling that he knew each individual animal in his wilderness by name.

After we had smoked together I slept until the late afternoon and then went to visit hooks with Zibi and Ankai Ho. We made a heavy haul. One fish was so large that I suggested shooting it, but Zibi warned me not even to mention such a thing because the finny creatures would be offended if they heard. They offered me all the trout but I accepted only four, since after I had fed two to the dogs I could not carry more without overloading my already weighted sled.

For the evening meal, the ancient hunter excised the large intestine of a fish and turning it inside out scraped the surface clean with his knife, afterwards cutting it into sections and laid them on some glowing coals. When they had burned on one side, he turned them over. Then he passed them around on sharpened sticks as the hors d'oeuvre for our dinner. We followed this with trout steaks so thickly encased in fat that the frying pans filled with oil as they sizzled on the fire. Then we lit our cigarettes and the old one pointed out the little toi-a birds that whistled in the trees near by. He asked me if they inhabited my homeland and I told him no. I sought out a magazine which in its advertisements had pictures of cities, trains, and other things that he had never seen. As I tried to explain these wonders, he only shook his head. He was fascinated by a full page in color of a necklace set with emeralds beside a matching pair of earrings. Jewelry he could comprehend, but when I told him what the pieces cost and how men worked to buy them for their women, he was incredulous indeed. To make my story reasonable I explained that such ornaments became the symbol of a great chief's wealth so that all would envy his ability to obtain these rare and beautiful treasures.

When I had finished he looked at me awhile, then raised his arms and turning in a quarter circle seemed to embrace the forest round about him. "*This* is beautiful," he said, "and if a hunter has his health he needs no more." Then very slowly he folded his arms and his head sunk down upon his breast. Everyone was quiet except the little toi-a birds, whistling in the tamaracks.

33

I FELT depressed in mind and somewhat constipated. In the box on my sled I found a tin of laxatives and took one while the Indians watched. They wanted to know the reason and when I explained, Susi Tucho's father asked to take one also. After I had given him a dose, the others held out their hands and I dispensed a pill to each which they swallowed with serious faces. The old man after a few minutes of silence looked up and spoke of something which made the others laugh. They said that he told them to be careful of the dogs and then to satisfy my curiosity explained enough for me to catch the common native joke. Dogs eat excrement and, crowding around in competition, often snap too close for comfort.

Deciding to leave that night, I gave the old one several plugs of chewing tobacco and he smiled, showing his worn but still abundant teeth. He was reputedly a shaman but would not discuss the subject when I asked him in the afternoon. Now as I said good-bye he half humorously announced that he would make a little medicine to speed me on my way. When I put dogshoes on my team Ankai Ho informed me that I could make them last much longer by fastening new ones over old. Then I thanked them for their hospitality and whirled off down the inlet following a course northeast across the bay.

After an hour of running fast I took my bearings on a distant mountain which lofty elevation soon proved to be a heavy snowdrift. When I tried to cut across it, I found it soft with floating ice in water underneath. Pulling, shoving, we worked foot by foot. My legs were soaking almost to the knees and nearly numb. The dogs fought for footing, Scotty tearing off his shoes. I could not synchronize their efforts and I was desperate from the cold. Ginger refused to work at all and in my fury I choked him with my hands. This treatment gained us nothing and as Whitey and Scotty tore out their hearts I took the dog chain and beat my steer dog. In this way we pulled through a hundred yards of slush and veered northward over smoother ice.

I removed my moccasins and socks and dried my legs, massaging the livid skin until it tingled evenly. Dressed again, we trotted on through the darker hours of night, Ginger occasionally jumping straight up in the air and twitching as though he had a fit. I feared that I might have caused him serious injury but by the time the morning sun had risen, he ran evenly and pulled his weight as though from long ingrained habit.

About five we turned up on a rocky island with some driftlogs on the shore but nothing save moss and willows grew there as far as I could see. My back pained and I went to bed to sleep until after three. Then I rolled over and slept two hours more.

When I finally arose, I fed the dogs two trout and broiled a big intestine on the coals for myself. It tasted fibrous and not unlike oysters that have partly dried from cooking. Afterwards I cut a spreader for the traces to replace the one we had broken the night before. Then I mended several harness straps which had torn half in two during our struggle in the drifts. This completed, I hitched the dogs and we moved out on the ice rounding the point the Indians call A-wi.

Setting a course due east, we followed along outside an ice pack that had jammed up more than twice my height. After the sun had risen above the cone-shaped hills bordering the shore, I found a gap in the pressure ridge and through it we hauled the sled. Inside there was slush and we headed for the beach to secure a supply of wood. After boughs were cut I stretched out in the open while a cold fog blew in from over the lake.

This day I slept fitfully, with frustrating dreams of a sled that had jammed in slushy snow. At times I would wake from my slumber only to slip into my troubled trance again. At last, I shook myself free and cooked some dog feed, eating part of it myself. Then I cut a pile of dry spruce sticks to fit into my tiny stove, and bundling them with a line, lashed them onto the sleigh along with two new poles for my tent.

I knew that the Indians who hunt beyond A-wi had joined with those at Alexi's camp on the foot of Bear Mountain. In consequence I had decided to make the traverse due north across the widest of the five great bays which constitute the Lake. Along the coast of this fjord country it was difficult even to pitch a tent whereas on the Barrens I should find natives of the eastern band.

We headed straight out from shore. After the first two hours the course worked deeper into an area of ice floes and water which had resulted from the surface snow melting and then freezing again. The sled would break through and wedge itself, Peter veering off when the straight pull seemed to gain him nothing. Then I would have to get out in the middle of the slop and add my strength to that of the dogs. Five times I changed my moccasins that night until, when I knew that I had only one dry pair remaining, I went barefooted into the slush. That experience I never repeated for I found the water against my flesh felt many times as cold and the ice ripped the heavy callouses on my soles like chips of glass. Once I had to portage the load, for heaving and tugging had almost torn the sled apart.

When we finally reached a continuous hard surface we were all bleeding from cut feet and legs and my hands were a gory mass of broken blisters. In the distance I could see mirages of land but after running toward them for a time, they only disappeared. We came to a high pressure ridge and followed along the edge some distance until we found a cleft through which we forced a passage. My back ached and I hated everything—dogs, ice, Indians, and life itself. At five-thirty I tied the headline to a block of snow and chained the dogs to it in the belief that if they shared my feelings I would never see any of them again. Then I stretched out on my sled and slept.

When I woke I could see no shore ahead and I built a little fire in the stove which although slightly battered, still clung between the runners. Just behind I had raised a tent pole and tied to it clumps of moccasins to dry, so that with the rising puffs of smoke one might have noted a resemblance to a tug-boat straining under tow of half a dozen barges. I reflected that in a week or two the snow would be melted and the slush absorbed, leaving glare ice on which to travel. Already there were oval mirrors of bare ice silvering in the sun, affording a surface which held no noticeable resistance for even a heavy sled when once the sled was started.

We pulled out early and trotted along in the lee of an ice pack for several hours, thus avoiding water-laden snowdrifts. Gulls came with us, circling while we stopped for the now frequent change of dogshoes. We had crossed the pack and moved shorewards half an hour when suddenly I saw the ax was gone. I stopped the sled and just stood there thinking. All the pain and suffering of the past week disappeared from mind like puffs of clouds slipping past the sun and one idea poured through my brain. When had I last seen that ax! Did I use it to chop a block of ice the night before? The more I thought the less was my certainty that it had been in my hands since I had cut kindling on the south shore of the lake. Surely it must have fallen off when we crossed the last pressure ridge.

Without a word to the dogs, I started walking back along our trail. Daylight had almost disappeared and all I noticed was the crispness of the snow, a certain sign that it would freeze hard before the morning. When I looked behind I could barely see the sled and I fancied for a moment that it might be just as well if I never saw the dogs again unless I found the ax. Mostly I did not think at all. I just walked with my eyes fastened to the trail.

I saw it glisten beside the tracks before I had gone a mile. As I grasped the handle with deep relief I had two thoughts—instantly I knew that I had checked my load every half hour or so when moving since I started driving dogs a thousand miles before and that with fair luck I could run a week without the ax at this time of year.

34

I RETURNED to the sled and called to the dogs to move again. We crossed more ice packs and finally reached the shore. Climbing a rock I looked around but could see nothing but a few islands with some trees in the distant background and Big Point faintly visible over thirty miles across the Lake to the southwest. We followed bare ice along the coast to the promontory and pulled up on the big drift of snow which still covered that end of land. Ginger who had worked least had been fed less than the others and was hungry. When he tried to steal some fish I beat him with a dog chain and he tried to bite me, his teeth grazing my leg. Then I hit him over the head with a stick.

We stayed two days while I went hunting without even seeing a ptarmigan. Then after repairing and repacking we moved out onto the ice with a southeast wind cutting across our flank. I felt fairly well again but my hands were stiff. The dogs had rested and seemed full of spirits except for Scotty, who had been sick to his stomach.

Running toward the end of the northeast arm of the lake we found no trails. The past week had seemed a lifetime. I could hardly remember when I had visited any Indians and I had little desire to see more human beings. As the Bay narrowed, I could distinguish high hills on the north shore and I turned directly toward them, camping far out on the ice in the early morning, just as a blizzard began to blow.

When I woke in the late afternoon it was still snowing and the gusts struck harder than before. I gave some dryfish to the dogs and with a piece for me to chew on crawled back into my eider down. Gradually the snow turned into sleet and by ten o'clock had stopped altogether, leaving the ice wet underfoot.

We reached the edge of the shore about midnight and turned left along it, walking through a thin layer of slush past several points of land. About two-thirty I saw several caribou and, taking my gun, waded down a bay behind them. My effort was useless for the fleet-footed animals ran off before I could come within shooting distance.

Our passage seemed to deteriorate as we moved on across the open arc of a shallow bay. I went ahead of the dogs, breaking a thin layer of ice which would not even support them, to say nothing of the sled. For several hours, we plunged on through water splattering up to my knees. The dogs' legs were cut and even their chests had turned red with blood where jagged panes of floating ice had pierced the skin. In the center of the arcing shore I could see some stumps on slightly sloping land so we turned toward them and pulled up on the bank in a blinding sleet. Finding a few sticks I made a fire and raised the tent over the sled. It was bitter cold when I crawled into my eider down.

By night it was still sleeting and I found myself in as miserable a situation as I had ever known. My clothes were soaked and everything around was wet. I stayed in the sleeping bag and read while the hours passed.

About three in the morning the snow stopped falling and I got up and looked around, glad to see the sunlight. I chopped some stumps and built a fire after which I repaired the front crossbar of the sled that had broken the night before. Then I fried some dryfish and boiled some cocoa, putting on dry underwear and socks to feel that everything was in order. I read awhile and then slept peacefully until evening.

The night was clear and cool. Some geese lighted in an open pool of water near by. I took my gun and with the first shot killed one and wounded another. I waded down the bay after the gander which I brought back and gave to Scotty, in part because he showed so much excitement over the kill and partly because I thought the change in diet might do him good. The other I boiled over an open fire beside a can of corn meal and we all had a feast at midnight.

I began to feel happy for the first time in a week. There were still quantities of water around but the slush was beginning to harden and I estimated that in an hour I might escape over a crust of dry ice. The wild geese were honking in numbers not fifty feet away, sounds which amused me and then disturbed my thoughts so I threw a stone at the birds but they were too much interested in mating to pay me any attention. I let them alone, and dreaming, lay back on the sled to watch the color of the sky begin to reflect on the thin wall of the tent. A flap fluttered in the wind and Neidja settled down on the end of the eider down.

"What are you doing here?" I said.

"You had better ask yourself what you are doing here," she answered, looking rather stern.

"I am having a wonderful time," I replied, feeling all at once as though the world were perfect. "Come and listen to the music. I have a complete orchestra of geese that plays the strangest symphony you ever heard."

My feelings were so exuberant that even she reacted to the mood but could not resist a petulant remark. "You did not seem to be so anxious to see me during the past week!"

"You should understand, Neidja. I was busy. In fact I had a very difficult trip during the past week. There simply was no time to think of women. Besides you know that you are the only one I love."

She blushed and turned her head away for a moment and in that instant I reached up and caught her hand, pulling her down beside me. The tent was hot as I drew her into my arms. She looked at me a moment and then closed her eyes as I kissed her wet lips.

"We should not lie here like this," she said, "you ought to get away from here right now!"

She struggled slightly but when I kissed her again she lay quietly.

"Surely you must know that I would not leave tonight if it is the last chance I ever have."

I did not wake until the rush of running water disturbed me. It was six-thirty in the evening and I looked outside the tent to discover a river flowing by. I was disgusted. At first I decided to move and then I thought by waiting the water might go down. By ten-thirty it was a torrent and I had to climb out and move the load to a drier place. Before midnight there were four inches of water sweeping under the tent and I hauled everything onto the sled and climbed on top. How miserable!

I read for awhile which eased my mind but then I had to drag the sled to the last dry spot. The water was bitterly cold and my feet ached for hours afterwards. At five o'clock I went out and waded in all directions. I found that I was in the middle of two impassable streams for I knew that if I soaked myself above the knees I would freeze to death as soon as the sun went down. I crept back on top of the load and waited but the water showed no sign of slackening. I tried to sleep but it was difficult to rest in the crash of those misery-reminding cataracts. They seemed to speak, to call to me. One sounded like a newsboy, hawking papers. My chest and back pained. "Pneumonia," I thought, "Suppose I die?"

Curiously, I only smiled; I was content. Neidja stroked my forehead and I fell asleep.

It was eleven at night when I awoke. The water was still running. I had taken the tent down and as I looked around I saw my four dogs facing me in a circle. They stood knee-deep in water unable to lie down, each gazing steadfastly at the sled to see what I would do. I tried to rest but with my head covered I felt their staring eyes. After awhile I could not stand it any longer and decided to move regardless of what might come.

It was midnight and I was hard at work. I put shoes on all the dogs and piled everything from the sled on a rock except the big box. My plan involved floating the almost empty sled a hundred feet or so from the shore where the runners would touch the ice and then carrying the remaining material on my back across the deep stream which hemmed me in, flooding the Lake beyond my vision. For all I knew this was perhaps a miraculous year and the breakup was on its way. In any event, the chance was worth taking rather than to watch my dogs die like fish in a trap.

We started out and in less than an hour I had the sled settled on clear ice covered by only three inches of water. It took more than twice as long to transfer all the equipment from our abandoned camp but I struggled in ecstatic desperation until by three o'clock the dogs were hitched to the load and we were moving steadily out onto the Lake. In about a mile we turned sharply to the right and raced for a distant point. I was excitedly happy. If there were fuel to burn, everything would succeed precisely as I planned. My body tingled from the exercise and all I needed was to dry my clothes. We traveled for several hours behind some small islands, and then as we rounded the point, we struck a perfect stretch of glare ice which formed a line just cutting off those miles of shallow bay and islands. We went on until we found a rising bank and pulling up, built a blazing fire from driftwood.

We were camped on the familiar muskeg which rose very gradually toward the mountains behind us while across the northwest bay of the Lake could be seen the faint outline of a hilly shore. Surveying the area which we had left, I realized that what I had done while under the attraction of dried stumps was to settle down in the mouth of a stream which drained the muskeg lands and had already flooded the narrow bay into which it emptied. It was certainly the one which the Indians named Te-le-dze-ge-di or Blood-flowing-down River because of a battle that they had fought there. Well, I would not be likely to play the fool for stumps again.

It rained during the day and I had difficulty in sleeping for the sound of running water gave me nightmares. Finally the rain stopped and I was able to dry my clothes with the combined help of a fire and a brisk wind. I checked my supplies and found that I still had one hundred and twelve dogshoes, a full week's supply thanks to Ankai Ho's advice on how to save them. I recalled that when the dogshoes were first made

I thought they would be a valuable addition more out of consideration for the dogs than any realization that a time would come when a lack of them alone could limit my movements. Between the trout and game birds there was little trouble to supply a sufficiency of food and I was learning however painfully the peculiarities of the spring melting. The surface of the dry ice was just beginning to take the form of a myriad unburned candle tops pressed tight together. The wicks were wisps of snow but the little cones of supporting wax were ice that could tear a dog's unprotected paws apart in half a day.

We ran on smooth ice far to the west that night and then cut off toward the white hills of the southern coast, eventually getting into wet snow drifts and rough ice before we reached the shore. Ginger had taken a beating for the last half mile and was sore because of it. Sometimes I wondered why he did not try to kill me when he had a chance but once out of the harness, unless exhausted, he wanted only to play. He would come to be hitched without any hesitation and then for hours pull with little persuasion until we met up with unusual difficulties. Thus confronted he would give up at a time we all needed his strength the most. It was I who hated then and nearly killed him, although on reflection I judged him as being only more childish than the others.

Scotty on the other hand still worked himself to the limit of his strength and I worried for his life. Yet on one evening, he would not come to the harness. What made him act that way I do not know but somehow his refusal symbolized a complete disintegration of our unity and I raged with a frustration shot through with fear. That was the only time that he was singled out for punishment and after I had hit him I almost wept when he reached up and licked my face.

Whitey likewise suffered only once. On a night while I was cutting wood, he stole some food from the sled. The other dogs protested and I caught him in the act. He groveled in shame and I hit him with the long caribou-skin whip. He did not move and only cried when the lash cut across his ears. Then I saw him cleaning his toes as I whipped him so I took the dog chain which shocked him considerably. I did not hit him hard for there was no anger in me. I never had been irritated at this dog who showed such consistent courage, such strength and loyalty. As for Peter, he had not seemed to be a dog for a long time. We argued a great deal and occasionally I punched him in the face.

The night we moved around Big Point back into our own arm of the Lake, I was struck by the sudden change in the character of the ice. Here the "candles" were no longer stuck together near the top but stood out like brilliants from a chandelier. There were also smooth open cracks through which I judged the ice to be still five feet thick.

We turned south and moving swiftly crossed the deep inlet which the Indians call "Where-they-swim-across," referring to the migratory bands of caribou, then pulled in to camp on a little point below a hill. I had stuffed myself by chewing pounded meat throughout the night and not feeling well, I did not sleep until late that afternoon. When I awoke it was almost morning, the sun at this time scarcely dipping below the horizon at midnight. It looked like a clear day for almost the first time in two weeks and as I saw some ptarmigan along the shore I decided to remain. I went after the birds but two gulls warned them so I shot the gulls and then went on and killed a ptarmigan, after which I put it on the fire to boil, beside a can of dogfeed. Even Scotty would not eat the gulls.

The day passed sleeplessly for me as I lay in bed, occasionally hearing the rumble of an ice jam around the point. At six o'clock I rose and cooked another meal, soon loading the sled and sliding down onto the level ice. The conditions for traveling were almost perfect and the dogs ran unceasingly while I, unable to compete with such speed, sat on the sled and looked at the pictures in a magazine. It seemed as though the dogs knew that they were heading straight for the Fishery about seventy miles away. The ice shifted to white, and then black, and back to "candled" again, but all served excellently for speed.

As we started to traverse the second large inlet along that shore, a heavy fog descended such as I had never seen. The dogs' hair bristled and they continually looked in all directions as if they were both lost and half-afraid. Peter had a shoreward drift which I continually called to him to check as I sighted from one little patch of snow or dark spot to another. For some reason he would not run in a straight line and at intervals I lost my temper and boxed him on the ears with bare fists. It was on such an occasion as I kneeled beside him that he snapped at me, not viciously but as a protest to my treatment. This surprised me more than anything that he had ever done before and with an instantaneous reflex action, I bit him on his white nose as hard as I could. He squealed and jumped away, looking at me in startled amazement which made me laugh. Then I shook hands with him and walked back to the sled.

The fog lifted as we approached the shore a few miles off Low Sand Point where we had made the traverse south twenty-nine days previously. Peter seemed to recognize the place and frequently sent sharp inquisitive glances toward the Fish Mountains and sometimes showed bursts of speed that made the sleigh whistle on the ice almost scaring Ginger who feared that in its momentum it might run him down. For almost five hours they ran that way, with scarcely a halt between, until we saw the cabins looming up in the sunshine ahead.

Weaving around the open water near the slough, we hauled the sled up on Big Rabbit Point beyond and I pitched the tent. It was still early for anyone to be around. The dogs who had run seventy miles in eleven hours seemed less tired than many a night before. As I patted them my eyes searched the village and then I saw the small unmistakable figure of Pierre waving a welcome from across the bay.